THE INFRA-WORLD

THE INFRA-WORLD

FRANÇOIS J. BONNET

Translated by
AMY IRELAND AND ROBIN MACKAY

URBANOMIC

Published in 2017 by
URBANOMIC MEDIA LTD,
THE OLD LEMONADE FACTORY,
WINDSOR QUARRY,
FALMOUTH TR11 3EX,
UNITED KINGDOM

Originally published in French as *L'Inframonde*.
© Éditions MF, 2015.

BRITISH LIBRARY CATALOGUING-IN-PUBLICATION DATA

A full catalogue record of this book is available
from the British Library

ISBN 978-0-9954550-4-7

Type by Norm, Zurich
Printed and bound in the UK by
TJ International, Padstow

www.urbanomic.com

CONTENTS

That which is known has value only by virtue of the dark. This cannot be otherwise. A thing known passes out of the mind into the muscles, the will is quit of it, save only when set into vibration by the forces of darkness opposed to it.

William Carlos Williams

UNVEILING

We tend to think of sight and hearing as faculties that are innate and immediate. Yet from the very start, they hold something back. What we see and hear cannot be entirely grasped by the intellect; it can never be completely assimilated. So what is it to apprehend the sensible? To feel, to touch, to see, to hear...? Each of the senses harbours an inviolable mystery, reserved for itself and inaccessible to the others. 'Between my sensation and myself, there is always the thickness of an originary acquisition, which prevents my experience being clear for itself,' as Maurice Merleau-Ponty says.[1] The primary modality of all sensation is vague, confused, or at least *uncertain*. Every sensation begins like this, at first—as a hazy emanation we can scarcely grasp.

The apprehension of the sensible is thus primordially *henotic*, to use Otto Weininger's term[2]—that is to say, it is undifferentiated, indiscernible. It is on the basis of this henotic apprehension that a qualified perception will be articulated, appearing only 'after the fact'. Weininger explains this passage from henotic apprehension to qualified perception in terms of the activation of a 'clarifying' process. This gradual unmasking, this evaporation of the uncertainty that enshrouds a sensation, is the very moment of the perception of an identifiable phenomenon—now truly grasped, through the fog of the sensible. So a sensation only becomes clear for one who senses it after it has been perceived, once it has broken through, been drawn back through the henotic veil, extracted from its own thickness.

---

1.   M. Merleau-Ponty, *Phenomenology of Perception*, tr. D.A. Landes (London and New York: Routledge, 2012), 224.

2.   O. Weininger, *Sex and Character* (London: William Heinemann, 1906), 84sq.

The identification of a sensation, its circumscription and objectivation, is therefore a *degradation* of the primary experience. It is founded on the principles of identity and recognition, activated under the assumption of a relation of 'sameness', and with recourse to the reic modality of the sensible. For the reification of a sensation, its 'thingification'—that is to say, its being allocated a place within the order of things—is an indispensable preliminary to its identification and its recognition. A reified sensation is thus degraded in so far as it is *conditioned*.

To condition the sensible is to place it *in* a new condition, to bestow upon it a reason for and a context of appearing; but it is also to place it *under* condition. This condition of possibility is that of its legibility, its univocity. All that is at stake in the elaboration of certainties on the basis of the sensible comes down to this: a univocal screening of sensations in pursuit of a clear perception. Thus clarification is the primary operation at work in the distancing of the sensible from itself, and the first step toward the accumulation of certainties. The now-clarified sensation is not clarified for itself, but *in order to function* in the service of some *usage*. Most of the time, in the context of 'everyday' perceptions, this clarification seems to cover its tracks as soon as it has occurred, since these perceptions appear to be instantaneous. And no doubt there is a period of apprenticeship during which, as we gradually mark out the field of known experiences, this clarification is *automatized*, so to speak.

Moreover, Weininger reminds us that clarification implies a distancing from what he calls the 'tonality of feelings'. The introduction of clear sensation into the known world is effectively a moment of apathy, a sort of crossing of the Styx whereby, leaving Hades behind, we rejoin the world of the supposedly living, a world that has always been functional, the world of utility. The clarification and characterization of sensation brings us home to the reassuring universe of certainties.

Inversely, a sensation we cannot manage to 'clarify' can engender a certain uneasiness, a panic which is that of the indefinable, the absolutely other. Perception breaks down, sensible experience fails to reveal itself, and facing this unknowable engenders a sense of anguish. The fear that invades us when we glimpse a furtive silhouette, a poorly-defined form lurking in the shadows, is a fear aroused by the potential threat such an unidentified presence may represent. But it is also the visceral fear of an unsolicited presence, one that does not belong to the known world; the fear of coming face to face with some abomination. This anguish, however, is not so much that of a phantasmatic projection, the imagining of some improbable monster (for what is essential to a monster is that it must de-*monstrate* itself and frighten us with its deformities) as that of the absence of any satisfactory projection: the anguish of being confronted by a nothingness for which we cannot manage to substitute any known thing.

Indeed, in virtue of this fact, we would be wrong to interpret children's night-time terrors as the result of excessive imagination. Contrary to popular belief, children do not have excessive imaginations. Upon hearing an unknown noise, spying a fleeting shadow, the adult will imagine a whole series of potential scenarios that might *explain* the phenomenon, bringing it back into the known world and rendering its existence probable. On the contrary, a child rapidly runs up against the limits of his imagination, then finds himself before the most radical, the most terrifying unknown. He finds himself at the gates of the infra-world, and there perceives the real danger of being snapped up by nothingness, of seeing the few certainties acquired during his early years shattered to pieces and sinking into the pitch-black waters of a groundless world. Against the structures of order and discipline, whether those of school or of the family unit, against the many strategies designed to initiate the child into the grown-up world (objects and coloured forms designed to 'awaken' him to the rigours of civic education or to the history of civilization), the terror of this blackness insinuates into the ear of the toddler a terrible promise: 'You will never know the world; the known world is already gone, it is collapsing around you. Its fictional limits are at breaking point, and the ensuing flood will carry you far, far away'.

In the neglected 1957 film *Night of the Demon* directed by Jacques Tourneur, it is not a child who has a 'Rendezvous with Fear' (the French title of the film), but a rational and experienced scientist, Doctor John Holden. Holden comes to London to participate in a conference on parapsychology with a view to expositing his theses on auto-suggestion, mass hysteria, and phenomena of collective hallucination. He intends to voice his scepticism regarding so-called 'paranormal' phenomena and related superstitions. But upon arrival he learns that his host, Professor Harrington, has died in mysterious circumstances. Everything seems to point to Doctor Julian Karswell, head of a local witch cult under investigation by Harrington, being the killer. Unwilling to accept that Harrington was the victim of a curse or an act of sorcery, Holden nevertheless finds himself caught up in the dark workings of Karswell's world. So much for the plot— and it must be admitted that the principal interest of the film does not reside therein.

What is striking in this story is that the demon's appearance (we see it three times) is always preceded by a deregulation of the senses. In Holden this manifests itself in visual distortions and fleeting hallucinations, both visual and auditory. Holden's meeting with the demon is particularly revelatory: the scientist, who will later explain that he had always sought to dismiss superstitions by deliberately provoking them (walking under ladders, crossing the path of a black cat), has broken into Doctor Karswell's house; in response to Karswell's warning not to go home via the forest, he responds that his only superstition is that he *always goes back the way he came*. Thus he once more enters the woods surrounding Karswell's estate. As he walks through the night, Holden feels his anguish mount as the shadows of tangled boughs create fleeting, disquieting forms. It is at this moment that the demonic apparition manifests itself, to his eyes only, and only partially, in the form of a sort of expanding orb of smoke.

The two other appearances of the demon are clearer, although in each case they are preceded by shots illustrating a confusion of the sensible (the play of shadows on a road at night, disorientation on a railway track, again at night). In fact, it was the producer of the film who insisted on the explicit appearance of the demonic monster, against the wishes of both Tourneur and his screenwriter. For what the film exploits above all is a fear of the unknown—which is based not on the representation of the monstrous, but on the ambiguity of sensations and a growing uncertainty as to whether the known world will survive.

Indeed, horror films often take advantage of this invisible fear, taking it for granted that terror comes in not at the moment of monstration, but that of suggestion. And even when the abject or the horrific is revealed, as in gore films for example, it is only, ultimately, so as to *make the viewer close their eyes*. The Danish director Lars Von Triers, in one of his habitual appearances at the end of an episode of his strange

TV mini-series *The Kingdom*,[3] following the final, particularly gruelling shot, explains that although he could try to scare the viewer with fake blood, it is only when he manages to make the viewer shut his eyes that he really gets to where he wants to, for 'true horror lurks behind closed eyes'.

The whole of *Night of the Demon*—apart from the adventitious appearances of the beast, of course—follows the same logic: that of an ungraspable horror which reveals itself only through suggestion, and is announced as a postulate but never actualised, precisely because it is always already there. For the rational man of science John Holden, the terror lies above all in the formlessness of the smoke that pursues him. A man who claims that his only belief is that he must go back the way he came—that is to say, very concretely, that he must fold his experience back onto the known (which is indeed the very essence of the rational approach to life)—is bound to be less frightened by the vision of the demon, which is a sensible manifestation, terrifying but certain, than by the indistinct existence of a living smog, exhaled from and sucked back into nowhere. The demonic already makes its appearance, already affirms its presence, in Holden, through the experience of a tremulous apprehension of the sensible that defies the known world.

For the sensible world cannot be identified with the known or knowable world. It becomes assimilated into this world on the sole condition that it is clarified—that is to say, integrated by a protocol of representation. Sensation alone, mute and fleeting, is never fixed anywhere. It is fuel for the perceptual imagination that will re-present it as clear and enduring. Qualified perception thus already belongs to the

---

3.   Original Danish title *Riget*.

order of representation. Sensation is only actualised as a constituent of the known world at the moment when consciousness grasps it, represents it.

We need not therefore distinguish between a perceptual imagination, an imagification of perception, and imagination as 'phantasy', as Husserl's typology would have it.[4] Imagination always participates in the recognition of a known world, even when it magnifies it and renders it marvellous. So the space of representation, however subversive it may be, is always a space of order, extending the coordinates of a known space and rendering it communicable. Sensation supposes, perception attests, and representation affirms. It is never a challenge to the world qua known world; it can pose a challenge only within that world.

Phantasms, dreams, wars, and loves may embrace or contest each other, but are coherent with and always rely upon an irrevocable centre: a known world superimposing itself over and replacing the space of representation.

*

As a child, when it was foggy, I believed it was my doing. Even more than that, it seemed to me that it was I and I alone, momentarily unable to extend my perceptual field, who had rendered the surrounding space opaque. An opacity that moved as I moved, gravitating around me, and yet was gigantic, often swallowing up a whole town and affecting the lives of thousands of people reduced to a state of semi-blindness.

---

4.   E. Husserl, Hua XXIII, *Phantasie, Bildbewußtsein, Erinnerung. Zur Phänomenologie der anschaulichen Vergegenwärtigungen. Texte aus dem Nachlaß (1898–1925)* (*Collected Works* vol. 11: *Phantasy, Image Consciousness, and Memory (1898–1925)*, tr. J.B. Brough [Dordrecht: Springer, 1980]).

A medusa-opacity definitively resonating with and through me alone. At that age, my internal states had an untrammelled influence over the real.

Instinctively, but without formulating the question clearly, I asked myself: 'What is the world if not a world *for me*?' It is a strange sensation to think of a whole world that is dependent on one sole and unique I, a world that ultimately exists only because I exist to sense it. Yet it must be admitted that I only apprehend the world through my own perceptual screen and that, if I cease to exist, then the world also ends, does not survive me, in so far as it is a priori impossible for me, after my death, to continue to perceive it as existing.

Such a relation to the world, forged on the irreducible frontier between a self and a universe that encircles it, finds particular resonance with the reflections of Arthur Schopenhauer. For him, the known world is only constituted as a *world* in so far as it is given to a subject who represents it to himself:

> 'The world is my representation':— this holds true for every living, cognitive being, although only a human being can bring it to abstract, reflective consciousness: and if he actually does so he has become philosophically sound. It immediately becomes clear and certain to him that he is not acquainted with either the sun or the earth, but rather only with an eye that sees a sun, with a hand that feels an earth, and that the surrounding world exists only as representation, that is, exclusively in relation to something. If any a priori truth can be asserted, then this is it [...].[5]

---

5.   A. Schopenhauer, *The World as Will and Representation*, vol. 1 [1819], tr. J. Norman, A. Welchman, and C. Janaway (Cambridge: Cambridge University Press, 2010), 23 (§1).

Through representation, or more precisely, in Schopenhauer, *representations* (intuitive representations, and then those belonging to the abstract order, the latter forming only one class, those of concepts, 'the sole preserve of man'), is deployed a conception of a world given only (via the subject-object dualism) to perception and which can only be affirmed as perception. From which Schopenhauer deduces that '[e]verything that can or does belong in any way to the world is unavoidably afflicted with this dependence on the subject and exists only for the subject. The world is representation'.[6]

In Schopenhauer representation is conceived as the primordial interface with the world, which establishes the world itself as such and, at the limit, is to be identified with the world, already forming the germ of its *comprehension*. For representations, even intuitive representations, are never of a purely sensible order. They are always part of a *reading*.

To set up the process of representation as an indispensable auxiliary to the apprehension of the world is thus to requisition the sensible as 'materia prima', as the original element in the formation of representations. What is more, this functionalisation of the sensible inevitably engenders its a priori pacification, by subjecting sensations to their representational destiny. For Schopenhauer subordinates the sensible to an understanding, anchoring it to a fundamental principle, that of causality:

> [...] [I]ntuition is, in every case, not based merely on the senses, but is intellectual: it is pure understanding-based cognition of the cause, given the effect, and hence it presupposes the law of causality. As a result, the possibility of any intuition, and with it

---

6.   Ibid., 24.

any experience, is wholly and fundamentally dependent on cognition of the law of causality [...].[7]

He thus ends up with a more developed proposition regarding the real world, one that involves the articulation of representation, the principle of causality, and the understanding:

> The world [...] presents itself completely and without reserve as representation, held together by the law of causality. This is its empirical reality. But on the other hand, causality exists only in the understanding and for the understanding. Thus the understanding is always the condition for the actual (i.e. active) world as such and in its entirety: without the understanding this world is nothing.[8]

According to Schopenhauer, then, as we confront the world perceptions are unveiled, veritable spatial and temporal markers transcoding received information into intelligible material. They are then constituted into imaginary coordinates so as to fabricate a representational web, aggregating together to take the form of a hypercomplex multidimensional 'image': the perceived world, the world as representation—that is to say, the real world.

The sensible unveiled and clarified is the sensible *used*, integrated into the dynamic of representation, a dynamic fundamental to the constitution of the world as it *is*. For all that, we must not neglect the fact that the sensible *permits* the world, and the world *permits* the sensible; in Schopenhauer's own words, 'it is true that space is only in my head; but

---

7.   Ibid., 34 (§4).

8.   Ibid., 35 (§5).

empirically my head is in space'.[9] This having been said, neither should we disregard the decisive consequences of a world given as representation. For we must not lose sight of the fact that the sensible, in so far as it allows access to the world of representations—that is to say, once more, to the real world—presents in itself, or rather becomes for itself, a major stake. For whoever controls the sensible, or at least directs it, in doing so de facto *manipulates* the representation of the world and thus the world itself. Mediation and mediatization of the sensible therefore play an essential role in the construction of the real.

9.   A. Schopenhauer, *The World as Will and Representation*, vol. 2, tr. E.F.J. Payne (New York: Dover, 1966).

ADMINISTRATION

Once clarified and represented, the sensible is destined to become an instrument of knowledge, falling under a reic, thinglike logic, a logic of use which it will now serve. The use of the sensible, consequent to its placing-in-representation, corresponds to its placing in the common, in a community, directly implying what Jacques Rancière calls its 'distribution':

> I call the distribution of the sensible the system of self-evident facts of sense perception that simultaneously discloses the existence of something in common and the delimitations that define the respective parts and positions within it. A distribution of the sensible therefore establishes at one and the same time something common that is shared and exclusive parts.[10]

This distribution is therefore fundamental, for it founds the space of the political, a space that is established on the basis of an aesthetic, defined by Rancière as a 'system of a priori forms determining that which is given to sense'. To which he adds:

> [I]t is a delimitation of space and time, of the visible and the invisible, of speech and noise, that simultaneously determines the place and the stakes of politics as a form of experience. Politics revolves around what is seen and what can be said about it, around who has the ability to see and the talent to speak [...].[11]

Such a distribution, or rather such an *enterprise* of the distribution of the sensible through its placing in common

---

10.   J. Rancière, *The Distribution of the Sensible*, tr. G. Rockhill (London and New York: Continuum, 2006), 12.

11.   Ibid., 13.

(community being both condition and finality of the distribution) supposes strategies and structures of power designed to operate it. In this way a whole administration of the sensible is established, one whose objective is indeed distribution, the arbitrage between those who have 'the ability to see and the talent to speak' and those who do not. Thus the administration of the sensible has an authoritarian function in so far as, via this distribution, it grants or creates authority. The one who has authority, who *makes* authority, is exactly the one to whom the community grants the qualification to speak, in virtue of a certain ability to see.

The administration of the sensible, as a structural harness facilitating strategies of distribution, intervenes at all stages of the process of the reception and exposition of the sensible. It therefore involves the execution of control or at least orientation of the sensible, with its intervention operating on three different levels.

The first action bears upon the sensible object—that is to say, the object qua producer or generator of sensations. Here the manipulation of the sensible potential of the object can take different forms, depending upon whether it secreted or banished, that is to say depending on its mode of *dissimulation*, from camouflage to travesty and cosmetic falsification. In this case what is given to be perceived is controlled through the *sensible alteration* of the object.

Such modifications are above all designed to modify the *aspect* of the object, with the aim of rectifying or suggesting the appropriate *response* to it. From military techniques of camouflage to the ritual finery and masks used by innumerable peoples of all continents, the management of the sensible modality of all objects, even before being a symbolic act, can be seen as an exercise of control over the sensations of the other, either so as to escape them or, on the contrary, so as to capture their attention, to fascinate them or at least to *fash-ion* them. Just as the stick insect moves and positions itself according to a vegetable mimetism in order to evade its pred-ators, so the peacock spreads out its great tail covered with the hundred eyes of Argus[12] so as to impress and frighten its enemy.

The second stage of the administration of the sensible, which is truly that of its distribution, is the moment of its mediatization and its 'routing'. The represented, perceived part of the sensible is *precisely* the *communicable* part, that is to say the sensible of which we can have a common experi-ence. Every community must a priori be founded as a com-munity of sensible experiences. It is in seeing and hearing the *same* things and in rendering them communicable, that is to say in *testifying* to them, that a sensible capable of distribut-ing a community can be constituted.

The media age will multiply the potentialities and reso-nances of sensible objects by considerably extending their zone of perceptibility. In return, it will submit them to its dif-fusion channels—that is to say, precisely, it will channel them and thereby control access to them. Yet we should not understand mediatization only in terms of its contemporary technological determinations. It has in all times been subject to attention and shaping, from the acoustics of sacred sites[13] to gardens in the French style. The modulation of the spaces and times of the presentation of the sensible (the ordered

---

12.   The legend has it that in homage to Argus Panoptes, killed by Hermes, Hera had his hundred eyes preserved in the plumage of her sacred animal, the peacock.

13.   See F.J. Bonnet, *The Order of Sounds*, tr. R. Mackay (Urbanomic: Fal-mouth, 2016), 27–30, 204–7.

given-to-be-seen of the garden, the given-to-be-heard of prayers magnified by reverberation) are thus above all, once again, auxiliaries of the manipulation of the sensible, determined as instruments for its control.

One of the most celebrated and accomplished examples of a modelling of space designed to distribute and administrate the sensible is Jeremy Bentham's project for the panopticon, first developed in 1786.[14] Bentham sets up in quite exemplary fashion a clear distribution between the one who sees and the one who is seen, between a permanent potential visibility and a constant invisibility. This creates a division between two classes of men, with the watchmen, representing free men, able to see at every instant every last act and gesture of the men of the second class: the inmates, men to be punished. The latter cannot see their watchmen, and therefore cannot *know* whether or not they are being watched.

But active control of the mediatization of perceptions goes beyond the development of those architectures within which the sensible circulates. Every action carried out on transmission channels, whether material or immaterial, participates in such strategies of control. This is the case with all techniques of obfuscation, parasitism, and filtering of the sensible, from the use of smoke to hide from the view of the enemy to the systematic jamming of protest demonstrations,

---

14.   The panopticon is a type of prison architecture in which an observation tower is placed in the centre of the enclosure, establishing potential direct visual contact with all of the cells, the concern being not so much for the watchman to see everything as to engender among the prisoners the feeling of being perpetually under surveillance. On this subject see Michel Foucault's essential *Discipline and Punish*.

as predicted, for example, by William S. Burroughs in his *Electronic Revolution*.[15]

The moment of mediatization is thus the moment of a channelling, a second-order conditioning where it is no longer the object itself that is altered, but its deployment within the space of the sensible. In each potential action made possible by the moment of mediatization (parasitism, anamorphosis, editing, reframing, perturbation of a signal, filtering) we are presented with the possibility of a moment of reformatting that is a potential obstacle to the *becoming* of the sensible. So this moment of the forming of the sensible is always doubled by that of the expression of some power or other.

Finally, there remains a third element subject to the coercive flux of an administration of the sensible. This 'element' is none other than the perceiving subject itself. As well as affecting the perceived object and the ways in which it is exhibited, strategies for the distribution of the sensible can also act upon its recipients. In this case, any means necessary will be seized upon in order to retain the subject's very faculty of perception under the empire of power—from the tactical use of drugs and toxins to the fanaticisation of masses, via (and this is doubtless the principal procedure) acculturation, education, and the disciplining of the ear and the gaze. Learning how to see, how to hear, knowing what to touch and when to touch it: this is what is implied by the administration of the sensible in its educative or disciplinary (depending on your

---

15.   In this text dating from 1970, Burroughs explains how to integrate audio-visual 'viruses' into political events. The use of tape recorders broadcasting riot soundtracks pre-recorded at demonstrations is given as an example. William S. Burroughs, *The Electronic Revolution* [1970] (Ubu editions), <http://www.ubu.com/historical/burroughs/electronic_revolution.pdf>. See Bonnet, *The Order of Sounds*, 210–11.

point of view) dimension. *It lays the groundwork for an ethics and a policing of the sensible.*

*

To control the sensible is thus to control the power—just as the Great Oz, through his avatars in the form of a giant head or a ball of fire, or by incarnating himself as a terrifying beast, imposes himself and reigns as master of the Emerald City, illustrating in exemplary fashion the causal link between the exercise of power and the dazzling of the senses.

And yet the world cannot be reduced to an Emerald City run by a charlatan (and the Great Oz is indeed, even by his own admission, a charlatan). The world has become more complex than this. As Michel Foucault writes, '[t]he old power of death that symbolized sovereign power was now carefully supplanted by the administration of bodies and the calculated management of life'.[16] There are no longer truly lords who draw their power from the fear that they provoke, the mortal danger they represent, with the armed wings of a royal and divine justice on their side. There are now structures of control, education, and discipline that accompany the individual through every aspect of his life. And these structures are not manoeuvred by other, separate entities, by individuals from outside or beneath the community, but by persons like any other, themselves subject to the corrections and channellings of these structures.

Power is nowhere, it is hardly crystallized by an identifiable ruling class any longer. But it is also everywhere, exercised by every individual locally and in the name of society as a

---

16.   M. Foucault, *The History of Sexuality 1: An Introduction*, tr. R. Hurley (New York: Pantheon, 1978), 139–40.

whole, depending on his duties and responsibilities—that is to say, according to the authority granted him. So that this distribution of an immanent power, molecularised through the multitude, boasts a total impunity, having no *identifiable* author to which it could be attributed. It exerts itself *in all innocence*. This slaving, in the cybernetic sense of the term, of the bodies and lives of individuals, is what Foucault identified with the term *biopower*.

In the epoch of biopower, the administration of the sensible has become a veritable biopolitics of perception, taking over the becoming of sensibilised bodies, declaring them by turns emitter-bodies and receiver-bodies of a system that it seeks to regulate. Like a magical illusion in the era of its technical reproducibility, the manipulation of perceptions finds its *reason* only in a domesticated sensible, of which it is a 'totalitarian' expression—totalitarian being understood here less in its classical tyrannical connotation than in terms of the fact that each person, qua individual, assumes a function of regulation and control in and for an administration of the sensible, and above all the fact that this administration founds a community in so far as it predetermines it in its totality.

This establishing of an administrated sensible has been precisely identified as the process of the domination of society by the logic of the *spectacle*. For the spectacle, as theorized by the situationists, is as follows: a *certain* use, a generalized use, of the function of the distribution of the sensible *in overt form*. We must not misunderstand this, however. At the very beginning of his foundational text *The Society of the Spectacle*, Guy Debord tries to dispel an ambiguity which, even so, would go on to generate an misidentification of the concept of the spectacle:

The spectacle cannot be understood as a mere visual deception produced by mass-media technologies. It is a worldview that has actually been materialised, a view of a world that has become objective.[17]

The spectacle, as a tautological stage of the sensible, becomes the moment of the disintegration of community. Part of a community founded on a sensible that is communicable and common, the society of the spectacle has become the space of a fission of community itself engendered by the production of the sensible. The sensible, qua received and communicated, is therefore not the principle of the community; it becomes, qua element produced by the community to address itself to each of its members as an individual, an agent of alienation. This in any case is what Debord suggests when he gives the very definition of the spectacle:

The spectacle is not a set of images; it is a social relation between people that is mediated by images.[18]

So it is not the proliferation of images and sounds itself that directly constitutes a society of the spectacle dominated by mediatized perceptions. It is, as Debord says, a vision of the world, or rather a manner of living the world, characterised by a blind fascination with perceptions, but also with techniques and means of generating or reproducing given-to-be-seens and given-to-be-heards, independently of all consideration of any possible principle of the integrity of the sensible. In such a

17.   G. Debord, *The Society of the Spectacle*, tr. K. Knabb (London: Rebel Press, 1983), 7.

18.   Ibid.

society, it is no longer a matter of directly seeing or hearing, but of continually producing and consuming the sensible:

> In societies dominated by modern conditions of production, life is presented as an immense accumulation of *spectacles*. Everything that was directly lived has receded into a representation.[19]

Debord condemns a world that has dissolved itself into representation, and evokes a world that would have been directly lived, or could be. Such a distinction should doubtless be considered alongside Benjamin's discussion of authenticity. For Benjamin, the authenticity of a sensible object, a work of art for example, is given through a co-presence, a community of space and time shared by the object and its observer. Once this co-presence is broken—that is to say, once the sensible object is mediatized in space and time—authenticity is lost.

Debord himself questions this theme of the alienation of perceiving subjects and the spatiotemporal distortions they encounter when faced with sensible objects become reproducible, now capable of infinite storage and accumulation. And yet situationist enterprises, particularly situationist research on the construction of situations or the creation of 'subversive' ambiences, attempt to seize the means of reconfiguration of the world as representation, rather than envisaging the recovery of a hypothetical relation to life and the world that would be direct, immediate, or, in other words, pure. Citing Marx, Debord recognises very well that 'men can see nothing around them that is not in their own image;

---

19.   Ibid.

everything speaks to them of themselves. Their very land-scape is alive'.[20]

On the basis of psychogeographical research, a 'study of the exact laws and specific effects of geographical environments, whether consciously organized or not, on the emotional behavior of individuals',[21] the situationists develop strategies that aim to intervene across the whole range of sensible human experience, and develop the concept of unitary urbanism:

> Unitary urbanism must, for example, determine the acoustic environment as well as the distribution of different varieties of food and drink. It must include both the creation of new forms and the détournement of previous forms of architecture, urbanism, poetry and cinema. Integral art, which has been talked about so much, can be realized only at the level of urbanism.[22]

Against a rationalised urbanism responding to the principles of utility, the situationists proposed a redeployment of the conditions of life according to affective principles, based on the observation of the experiences and emotions that every place generates. Confronted by the reign of 'appearance', which makes of every *sensible surface a signifying surface* (whether that of road markings, advertising hoardings, traffic lights, or pavements, rumble strips, road signs, all designing and signing spaces of circulation, marking out sensible space), they

20.   G. Debord, 'Theory of the Dérive', in K. Knabb (ed.), *Situationist International Anthology* (Bureau of Public Secrets, 2006).

21.   G. Debord, 'Report on the Construction of Situations', in Knabb (ed.), *Situationist International Anthology*.

22.   Ibid.

sought to break through the crust of the administrated sensible:

> Considered in its own terms, the spectacle is an *affirmation* of appearances and an identification of all human social life with appearances. But a critique that grasps the spectacle's essential character reveals it to be a visible *negation* of life—a negation that has taken on a *visible form.*[23]

Thus the object of the situationist critique is indeed the modes of distribution of the sensible, the ways in which the empire over sensations is expressed and organized; but also the manifestations of this domination, and the specific modality of the spectacle, in which the exposing of power over the sensible is already a moment of its exercise. The spectacle has become a *generalised intrigue, in the era of biopower*.

*

But there is another distribution of the sensible, prior to that which orchestrates its introduction into a community, prior to that which conditions the body through the mediatization of the sensible. There is a distribution prior to distribution and which overprints it; an intimate distribution that operates in the field of sensations themselves. For perception itself erects an invisible wall between the perceived sensible and the unperceived sensible.

What is more, this infra-sensible is just as much that which is subtracted from perception as that which crouches beneath the tar of roads screened by visual signals, its absence and muteness seemingly defying a garrulous,

23.   Ibid.

proliferating sensible which, once it is present, beckons to us with its interminable signs. The sensible is never neutral, never mute. It speaks, it ceaselessly spins stories, fabricates fictions, spreads out over all surfaces, or over *the* surface of the represented world, making of the space of the sensible a *pan-signifying* space, a *totally legible* space.

Even prior to the foundational act of a politics, then, the distribution of the sensible is itself a distribution between sensible and infra-sensible. Each of us carries out our own distribution within ourselves, distinguishing perceived sensations, those we represent to ourselves and which constitute the known world, from those that evaporate, that are forgotten before even having been grasped, and are condemned to live a half-life, stillborn—that is to say, quite exactly, destined to remain in limbo.

VACILLATIONS

For long he believed he was still striding through the forest, in the numbingly warm wind, which seemed to blow from all sides and move the trees like snakes, following the barely visible blood-trail of the regularly pulsing ground in an always similar twilight, alone in the battle with the animal. In the first days and nights, or were they only hours, how could he measure the time without the sky, he even asked himself sometimes, what might be under the ground, which beat in waves underneath his footsteps so that it seemed to breathe, how thin the skin over the unknown thing beneath and how long it would hold it back from the entrails of the world.[24]

In this incomparable text by Heiner Müller, the exact title of which is *Heracles 2 or the Hydra*, Heracles sets out in search of the many-headed monster in hopes of vanquishing it. Walking for some indefinite period through a shifting, living forest which transforms as he moves through it, Heracles suddenly *realises* that what he had taken for a forest was, itself, already, the hydra:

[...] [He] understood, in the rising panic: the forest was the animal, for some time now the forest he thought he was walking through had been the animal, which bore him in the tempo of his steps.[25]

This tipping point, this moment of discovery where the ambivalent, unstable, and strange impression of being in an unknown

---

24.   H. Müller, 'Heracles 2 Oder Die Hydra', in *Werke 2: Die Prosa* (Berlin: Suhrkamp, 1999). Translation by Dennis Redmond.

25.   Ibid.

world gives way to the conviction, overwhelming and absolute, of already being upon the monster, is not exactly a moment of relief. It has that vertiginous force that turns one's stomach. But this jolt is not merely the effect of a retroactive emotion, a realisation of having misunderstood. It is also provoked by the violence of a return to the fixed world of certainties, as a definitive end is put to all exploration of the sensible, all specu-lation, and the senses are confiscated and reassigned to inter-facing with the known world, no longer destined for anything but the battle to come:

> Something like a lightning-bolt without beginning or end described a white-hot current of electricity through his veins and nerve-stems. When the pain overwhelmed the controls over his bodily functions, he heard himself laugh. It sounded like relief: no more thought, that was the battle. Adapting to the move-ments of the enemy. Avoiding them. Anticipating them. Meeting them. Adapting oneself and not adapting. Adapting by not adapting.[26]

As testified to by Heracles's emotions, panic finally gives way to relief, the relief of a world without fog which is a clarified world where phenomenological investigation, to use Michel Guiomar's term,[27] is banished in favour of a logic of things, the functional logic of a world in good order.

A world in order is a world of the ordered sensible, a world where things have their place, where those that exist are pre-sent and those which do not exist are absent. It is a world

---

26.   Ibid.

27.   See M. Guiomar, *Principes d'une esthétique de la mort* (Paris: José Corti, 1967).

where every thing responds to a use, and where nothing
remains to be explored or revealed. An available world, favour-
ing action and apprenticeship, a world of relief where ambigui-
ties become marginal and do not interfere with the perennial
nature of things.

The situation thus *clarified*, Heracles himself becomes
reducible to the functional economy of his warrior body, to a
decomposition of arms/legs/swords/axes themselves cou-
pled to the infinite heads of the hydra. There is no longer any
thickness, any uncertainty. All that remains is a flat surface of
functional exchanges putting the world in order through
actions.

A world in order: this, on the contrary, is what falls apart
for Lord Ewald. In Auguste de Villiers de l'Isle-Adam's tale *The
Future Eve*, Ewald, having accepted the proposition of the
scientist Thomas Alva Edison, plunges into a world that is too
vast, too arbitrary, and which can only occasion fear. Edison
proposes to create an android creature in the image of Ewald's
lover Alicia Clary, whose beauty, as great as that of the Venus
Callipyge, is equalled only by her spiritual vacancy. Observing
Ewald's despair, exacerbated daily by the infinite distance
between the young woman's exceptional appearance and the
commonness, even vulgarity, of her personality, Edison offers
to reproduce his friend's beloved identically, but this time
endowed with a mind to match her beauty.[28]

Having succeeded in his project, before unveiling the
gynoid (or 'android', according to Villiers), Edison proposes
that Ewald meet with the original Alicia Clary one last time, to
take his leave of her. Startled by this final meeting, Ewald,

---

28.   A. de Villiers de l'Isle-Adam, *Tomorrow's Eve*, tr. R. M. Adams (Chicago:
University of Illinois Press, 2001).

rediscovering Alicia in a new light in which her spiritual quali-
ties are finally revealed, and finding himself more amorous
than ever, no longer wants the copy. But it is then that Alicia
reveals to him that the true Alicia has already left, and that the
Alicia he is seeing and holding in his arms is she, the Android.
Feeling himself 'insulted by Hell itself', Ewald makes an examination of the creature:

> He took her hand: it was the hand of Alicia! He breathed her
> perfume; his eye measured the curve of her bosom; it was cer-
> tainly Alicia! He looked deep into her eyes; they were the very
> same eyes...only her expression was sublime! Her dress, her style,
> even that handkerchief with which she silently wiped away two
> tears that coursed down her lily cheeks—it was the woman
> herself...but transfigured! Become at last worthy of her own
> beauty, her real identity finally brought to life![29]

Certainly, in this tale, the new Alicia is animated by the mag-
netism of the mysterious Any 'Sowana' Anderson, a cataleptic
character cared for by Edison, and whose power of suggestion permits her to 'inhabit' the steel body of the automaton.
Nevertheless, the total artifice represented by the Android
operates an *exact* deception of Lord Ewald's sensations.

At this precise moment of discovery, revealing the possibility of the perfect—even more than perfect—reproduction
of natural reality, Ewald cannot help but be gripped by an
impossibly doubled sensible reality, and by virtue of this aban-
don forever a certain feeling of truth, or at least of conviction—he loses a certain confidence in his faculties' ability to
apprehend the world as it is.

---

29.   Ibid., 193.

What is revealed across these two texts is that a sensible confusion, an error in apprehension, is irrevocable, in the sense
that its being corrected does not annul the preceding sensible
relation, which remains constitutive of the perceiving subject
and the world as he knows it. For Heracles, the hydra will
always be superimposed upon the living forest he has ardu-
ously traversed, and for Ewald the Android will always be the
true Alicia. For the protagonists, and in them, these were
authentic moments; and although these moments subsequently yielded to another reality (the forest is the monster,
this Alicia is an automaton), they are not thereby invalidated.
Heracles leaves the forest of sensations to join combat against
the beast, at a moment when it is no longer time to feel but to
act. Ewald prolongs the illusion, adopts the simulacra, by
deciding to live with the automaton. He opts to bracket out
the terrible truth that 'she' is a machine so as to be able to live
out his love and veneration fully, thus taking leave of a certain
world, the one he thought he knew, a *world of certainty* (but,
as the tale has it, Ewald can never truly enjoy this *impossible*
situation: he will drown along with Edison's creature, as the
ship that was bringing her back home with him sinks).

At the moment of the shift between these two phases of
perception, in both Heracles and Ewald we observe a vertiginous feeling, a sort of stomach-turning sensation that is also
transmitted to the reader. At the moment of the animal trans-
figuration of the hydra-forest, which transfers the hero from
an indistinct space onto the very body of the monster, or that
of the dehumanisation of Alicia, which is followed by the all-
too-human rehumanisation of the animated Android, other
sensible realities are revealed, realities either underdetermined
by confusion (Heracles plunging the hydra into the vegetable

kingdom of the forest) or overdetermined by reason (the recourse to artifice in *Future Eve*).

If, as Schopenhauer suggests, the world is representation, then it lies within the power of man, by manipulating representations, to modify the world qua world for himself; to reconstitute it, so to speak, in an idiosyncratically resonant form, a world radiating forth in itself and for itself.

Such an artificial construction enters into dialogue with the world of certainties, producing sensible artefacts which are superimposed upon it and replace it, incrementally, so to speak, with supplementary sensible layers that depend no longer on Nature, but on the genius of man. In this way artifice serves to exorcise the sensible world qua world to be suffered, metamorphosing it into a controlled dream world—that is to say, a world that is recognised, but not authentic.

So what Baudelaire salutes as the 'brutal and enormous' magic of dioramas is nothing other than that which brings a certain relief, a certain *jouissance* felt in the presence of this omnipotence afforded by the mastery of artifice. And in fact this magic stems from the expressive potentialities of a reconstruction of the sensible that speaks, that speaks to us and thus reinforces our position in the world, legitimating our place within it not so much by validating the hope that the world should, of itself, correspond to our expectations, as by rendering it *plastic* before our desires.

In *Against Nature*, Joris-Karl Huysmans invents a character who was to become the emblematic figure of fin-de-siècle decadence. In the following passage, Huysmans reveals one of the typical procedures to which Des Esseintes habitually turns in order to enjoy the multiplicity of the sensible world without having to actually engage with it:

There, by salting your bathwater and mixing into it, according to the formula given in the Pharmacopeia, sodium sulphate, hydrochlorate of magnesium, and lime; by taking from the tightly closed, screw-topped box, a ball of twine or a tiny piece of rope specially purchased in one of those huge ship's chandlers whose enormous warehouses and basements reek of sea-tides and sea-ports; by sniffing those fragrances which will still cling to the twine or piece of rope [...] finally, by listening to the moaning of the wind gusting under the arches of the bridge, and the rumbling of the omnibuses as they cross the Pont Royal just a few feet above you, the illusion of being near the sea is undeniable, overpowering, absolute.[30]

Des Esseintes's decomposition of sensations participates in a reification of the sensible whose primary aim is *jouissance*. But if allowing one's sensations to fall back onto artificial procedures is above all a way to become the demiurge of a new world erected for one's own pleasure, it is also, in a certain sense, to pledge allegiance to the real world by augmenting it with an imaginary part which, even as it relativises the need for authenticity, secures its grip on a world fashioned by representations. No point in going to the seaside, Des Esseintes demonstrates, if the combination of sensations it provokes can be artificially reproduced on the banks of the Seine.

The artificial world can thus be apprehended as a 'fabrication of images which impose their evidence upon the senses, which make themselves believed in, and which in doing so *lend flavour to life*, and perhaps to God'.[31] In this way, then, it

---

30.   J.-K. Huysmans, *Against Nature*, tr. M. Mauldon (Oxford: Oxford University Press, 1998).

31.   M. Fumaroli, preface to J.-K. Huysmans, *À Rebours* (Paris: Gallimard Folio, 1977), 36.

appears as a simulacra, a phantom from which emanate colourful, picturesque vapours, aesthetic curiosities.

Nietzsche, a man of his time and a keen reader of Schopenhauer, detects a contemplative character, a preponderance of the senses, among his contemporaries—'Today all of us are believers in the senses', he writes in *The Gay Science*[32]—in parallel with a defiance toward ideas. Inverting the order between ideas and the senses, he shows that it is indeed the *sensible reading* of the world that produces knowledge and reaffirms the known world, while nuancing and indefinitely augmenting it:

> We who think and feel at the same time are those who really continually *fashion* something that had not been there before: the whole eternally growing world of valuations, colors, accents, perspectives, scales, affirmations and negations.[33]

Des Esseintes, the thinking-and-feeling persona par excellence, commits himself entirely to such contemplation, assuming his status as creator *qua spectator* of the known world so as to accede, by way of artifice, to illusion, to the autosuggestion of a dream world.

On the contrary, it is an inversion between fictional and phantasmatic worlds that is revealed in Fernand Fleuret's novel *Jim Click, or The Marvellous Invention*—a story, moreover, that reprises the theme of the perfect automaton in almost identical manner to that employed by Villiers de l'Isle-Adam.[34]

---

32.   F. Nietzsche, *The Gay Science*, tr. W. Kaufmann (New York: Vintage, 1974), 332 (§372, 'Why we are no idealists').

33.   Ibid., 241–2 (§301, 'The fancy of the contemplatives').

34.   F. Fleuret, *Jim Click*, tr. B. Stableford (Tarzana, CA: Blackcoat Press, 2015).

The story of *Jim Click* takes place in England on the cusp of the nineteenth century. Doctor Click, benefitting from a situation that provides him with a comfortable living, spends all of his time on a peculiar project: making a perfect copy of his childhood friend Admiral Gunson by inventing an automaton identical to him in every way. But the night when Doctor Click presents the Admiral's mechanical double to him proves disastrous: late on a very drunken evening, in an impromptu boxing match between double and original, the automaton deals the admiral a deadly blow.

Drunken and panicked, Click decides to switch the two, hiding his friend's lifeless corpse in a barrel. The next morning, however, Click is caught unawares and finds himself obliged to embark together with the automaton-Admiral on a major sea campaign. And so the story unfolds, with the subterfuge threatening to occasion all manner of mishaps—but the copy is not discovered. With its few recorded phrases typical of the taciturn admiral, it deceives everyone. During an epic naval battle, the automaton receives a bullet that ought to be deadly, thus making the Admiral's death official and freeing Click from his deception. But against all expectation, in a fit of guilt Doctor Click reveals his invention, and by the same token the murder of the Admiral by his machine double, in a letter addressed to the King. At first nothing happens: upon returning home, he is taken for mad and interned, the authorities having informed the mayor of his extravagant letter. He writes his memoirs, and commits suicide.

Just one man, J.H.D. Robertson, takes an interest in this story, and decides to go and explore Doctor Click's cellar where the original Admiral's body is supposedly hidden. If it were to be found, it would prove the truth of the Doctor's story. Arriving on the scene, Robertson, along with Doctor

Vilkind, Click's psychiatrist prior to his death, and Mr. Clark, the guardian of the house, does indeed find a body; but Clark swears that it is not the Admiral's. To his great astonishment, the relic stored in the barrel is that of the automaton. So Click had locked up his own creation, taking it for the Admiral's corpse. The man-machine that Click had accompanied to sea, that man who spoke only rarely and always with the same words, was not the automated creature—despite sharing all of its traits—but an actual human being.

This discovery discloses a reality so revolting that it will lead to the madness and suicide of Robertson's two compan-ions. Here we find the same scandal as that discovered by Lord Ewald when Alicia is revealed to him as an android, even if it goes in the opposite direction to that of *Future Eve*: the discovery of a truth implying a potential equivalence that pro-vokes a confusion of sensations between the world of cer-tainties and that of machinations.

Jim Click believed that he had hallucinated the authentic in the automaton, but in fact he had revealed the artifice in the human. The construction of sensible certainties rests upon a constant process of mystification and imposture, revealing the ambiguity of any recourse to artifice.

For artifice is ambivalent. It is the instrument of a confu-sion of the sensible, even when it is designed to bring about or extend aesthetic relief. It harbours an excess which, in this way, reveals the *more-than-perfect* yet ultimately just as fac-titious character of naturalist representation. Both one and the other (the artificial and naturalism) are procedures that place the sensible in the service of functions motivated by the a priori affirmation of a world—that of idiosyncratic imagina-tion in the case of artifice, that of objectivity and immutable laws in the case of naturalism.

In drawing on this procedural commonality, the artificial imperils a relation to the real mediated by naturalist representation, by revealing in it a similitude, an artificial character. Artifice thus always denotes an insecurity: the possibility of its insinuating itself into a real world and overprinting itself on this world as an unsolicited presence, liable to compromise the generalised enterprise of clarification. And yet the world of utility can also be the dupe of artifice, absorbing it and initiating an equivocal cohabitation. It is in this way that the marriage of the artificial and naturalism has been celebrated through the *augmentation* of the real.

Augmented reality is indeed the more and more profound objectivation of perceptual reality, the adjunct to sensory and cognitive artifices that increasingly render the surrounding world a world to be read, to be *decoded*. Thus artifice authorises a relation to the world that is *more than human despite being human*.

For artifice exceeds the human, fundamentally. It sweeps a broader spectrum, reaching beyond and falling short of the human. Immersive artificialities, from those evoked in *Against Nature* to those of *Sensorama*, the first multi-sensory machine offering the experience of a virtual reality (1956), have always been interwoven with a naturalist apprehension of the real in a spirit of simulation, making of artifice, ultimately, an extension of the human sensorium. The elaboration of a virtual space is understood as the assumption of an actual, real world. The virtual never shows us a reality other than the world, but instead another representation of the real world, extended in and by the imagination. And yet artifice *as such* has always harboured a modality that properly exceeds man and the limits of his experience of the sensible world, instilling a sort of disquiet.

*

In a short and celebrated text dating from 1810,[35] Heinrich von Kleist, through the mouth of Monsieur C..., the first dancer of the Opera, affirms the superiority of puppets' dances over those of humans—for the dance of puppets does away with all physical, terrestrial constraints. It is suspended in the ethereal in-between. The steps of the dancer who must pose and repose as he falls back to the ground are not really dancing, whereas suspended puppets never stop dancing, and 'only *glance*' the ground.[36]

One might object that puppets have no consciousness and therefore *do not dance*. And yet the spectator sees them dancing. And their movements are perfectly neutral, in the sense that *their soul is not in them*, to use Kleist's expression. Such a dance is, so to speak, 'pure', incapable of affectation.[37]

Here artifice appears as a promise of perfection, and again we discover the 'overwhelming and absolute' character of Des Esseintes's sensible machines. The recourse to artifice is thus distinct from direct, natural experience in so far as the experience produced is fabricated and can be re-invoked at leisure. Through the intervention of artifice the apparatus of the sensible becomes operatory, since it is abstracted from all hazards or contingencies. Similarly, the dance of the puppet approaches perfection in so far as its movements do not submit in the least to the direction of a consciousness proper.

---

35.   'The Puppet Theatre' [1810], in *Selected Writings*, ed., tr. D. Constantine (Indianapolis and Cambridge: Hackett, 2004), 411–16.

36.   Ibid., 413.

37.   'For affectation occurs, as you know, whenever the soul (*vis motrix*) is situated in a place other than a movement's centre of gravity.' Ibid.

To abstract from contingencies—this is also what Evelyn Habal, the pitiful character in *Future Eve*, discussed above, seeks to do. Habal, an apprentice dancer, is a past mistress in 'the art of pleasing', camouflaging her sickly and graceless constitution through all manner of technique and artifice, and thus transfiguring herself into a pretty child with long red hair. The fact that Edgar Anderson, a childhood friend of Edison who is also the narrator of the tale, falls under the spell of this creature, compromising his marriage in the process, is explained not so much by the success of Miss Habal's enterprise of camouflage as by its failure.

For Anderson at first felt no attraction to the young woman. Moreover, '*he didn't even know why* this girl was slightly displeasing to him, physically speaking'.[38] It is only later, as the evening goes on (and with the help of champagne) that he will become interested in her,

> simply [...] because of the *effort* involved, when he tried, by rousing his sensual imagination, to overcome an initial aversion to the general appearance of Miss Evelyn, by setting before himself the possible pleasure of possessing her—he was seduced, in short *by the aversion itself*.[39]

The desire that awakens in Anderson is thus indeed induced by artifice, not in so far as the artifice bridges the gap of Evelyn Habal's deficiencies, but rather in so far as it *reveals them by concealing them*. Something persists that generates unease, but also fascination.

---

38.   Villiers de L'Isle-Adam, *Tomorrow's Eve*, 104.

39.   Ibid., 134.

Just as the puppets, executing a simulacra of dance, *invent* an overhuman dance, so Miss Habal's 'beauty' is a monstrous beauty, inspiring both disgust and lust, a beauty that lies on the fringes of humanity.

And the fringes of humanity are indeed where artifice dwells, as it transfigures the false, adulterates the real, but always retains it as the reference point of its actions. A non-place, an engulfing power like that of a black hole, where everything, at any moment, could be dislocated because of its equivalence, because of the indistinction between what is given and what is constructed, fashioned.

Automata and puppets thus draw their 'life' from that non-place of perception that is the illusion of facticity. The uneasiness that the automaton can produce lies not in effective resemblance, but precisely in persistent dissemblance. For the automaton does not create unease by force of simulacra. Rather it is its inert, vain presence that is troubling. It is its inutility that is properly scandalous, an inutility that projects it out of the world, even while it is right there in the world.

What is to be done with an automaton, a mannequin, with its reasonless, functionless limbs? This is a problem that Hans Bellmer has traversed. In creating *La Poupée*, a female adolescent made of wood and papier maché, Bellmer undertakes a series of declensions and representations of a human body become modular, where each limb, each part, harbours a potentially autonomous existence. These 'Variations on the Montage of an Articulated Minor'[40] certainly give onto phantasms, onto the desire for an object-body. And yet Bellmer does not show his creature in suggestive poses—or, more exactly, he never quite succeeds in doing so.

---

40.   See *Revue Minotaure* 6 (Paris: Albert Skira, December 1934).

Of course one can make out in these photographs elements of a fetishistic imagination (the varnished shoes, for example, or the carpet beater in the foreground of a photo announcing an inevitable spanking), and yet these elements seem to always hold back, and it is instead a feeling of impotence that transpires, along with this question which ceaselessly returns: 'What is to be done with this doll?' Because the doll forestalls all usage, however perverse. Although it evokes the human, although it figures a young girl, it does not simulate one. Its artificiality is plain to see, and Bellmer seems not to know what to do with it, or dare not. His relation to the doll, via its artificiality, seems to crystallize around a sterilisation of desire. So he decides to play with it not by way of resemblance or pretence, but through an extrapolation of its body, an exploration of its body via a becoming-other.

In his *Games of the Doll*, a photographic series staging a new, more mobile, more malleable wooden girl in various corporeal situations and configurations, Bellmer has the creature's limbs proliferate, forming clusters, so that two pelvises merge into one torso. From frame to frame, the body of the puppet, designed for nothing other that to submit to the flux of mutations, is transformed—or more exactly seems to seek an autonomous form, a raison d'être other than 'for nothing'.

The path running from *The Doll* to end with *Games of the Doll* is indeed the path of metamorphoses, along which the body is fractalised, entirely losing its primordial raison d'être, losing the use of its limbs and their functions, displacing them, rendering them, so to speak, decorative. Beyond desire, the puppet then becomes a blasphemous object that bears within itself a terrible promise, a promise that its entire unsolicited presence harbours in germinal form: that the ground is about to open up beneath our feet.

A similar experience of the gulf of artifice is suffered by Nathaniel, the young man shattered by the figure of the Sandman,[41] a demonic character that had traumatised him as a child. Subsequently Olympia, an automaton-creature, will provoke the fascination of the same Nathaniel, who throughout his life is unable to resist the drift of autosuggestion and auto-persuasion, having been poisoned as a young child by the impressions left by the horrific Sandman. If Freud saw in 'The Sandman' a perfect illustration of 'disquieting strangeness', it was because the Sandman, with his latent threat that he will pluck out Nathaniel's eyes, reveals himself as a castrating figure.

Although he refuses to limit the disquieting strangeness to a frightening phenomenon that leads back to 'what is known of old and long familiar',[42] Freud says nothing of the strange fascination Nathaniel feels for the automaton Olympia, or of that which finally seals his fate—namely, *his belief* in the Sandman.

Two successive reversals render Nathaniel's existence utterly impossible, two reversals which throw the coordinates of the real into disarray so definitively that the young man himself no longer knows how to exist in the world.

The first reversal takes place when Nathaniel, still a child, realises that the phantasmatic monster, the Sandman, is in fact an individual he recognises, a household employee, the lawyer Coppelius. As he himself admits, nothing could have incarnated the Sandman more odiously for Nathaniel than

---

41.   'The Sandman', in E.T.A. Hoffmann, *Tales of Hoffmann*, tr. R.J. Hollingdale (London: Penguin Classics, 2004), 85–125.

42.   S. Freud, 'The "Uncanny"', in J. Strachey (ed.), *Standard Edition of the Complete Psychological Works* (London: Hogarth Press, 1953–1974), vol XVII, 220.

Coppelius, for there is less horror in an imaginary monster from fairy tales than in a real man who sows suffering and misfortune. Thus the child's terror folds back onto a known field of experience, a familiar world where the nocturnal part of this repugnant character with whom he must continue to cohabit is revealed in the light of day. For many years past a rampant horror has come to dine in his family home.

The second reversal, which finally sets the seal on the young man's 'madness', takes place when the fascination he feels for the young Olympia gives way to an incurable delirium when he discovers her for what she is: an automaton. Because of the absence of alterity *that she produced*, this idealised companion had become the ideal complement for a young solipsistic man who had always experienced the world as a threat. For, far more than a castration complex, Nathaniel's psychosis resides in the alterity of a world replete with threats, including that seminal, inaugural threat of the Sandman. 'His power is only your belief in him', as his young fiancée, Clara, had wisely predicted.[43]

In Hoffman's tale, the link between these two shocks is articulated around Nathaniel's eyes, eyes which the Sandman/ Coppelius threatened to pluck out and which will be found again in the orbits of an automaton, in a strange doubling, this threat never having been carried out. Nathaniel has been blinded by his own gaze, as was Narcissus by the watery looking-glass that sent him back to himself in a different form.

The threat of the world connected with the persecutory presence of the Sandman is thus intimately linked to the way in which the young man perceives his surroundings, a deformed perception that combines partial experience and blindness.

---

43.   Hoffmann, 'The Sandman', 103.

And once again, Clara had foreseen this terrible disposition in her lover: 'all the ghastly and terrible things you spoke of took place only within you, and [...] the real outer world had little part in them.'[44]

*

This phrase could have been taken from Jeff Nichols's film *Take Shelter*. It would have been spoken by Samantha LaForche to her husband Curtis. For Curtis LaForche is prey to great disquiet. He dreams of great storms, torrents of oily rain. In his nightmares his family attack him and wish him ill. But what truly afflicts him is that these bad dreams persist, their impressions haunting his days, during his time with his family and at work. He begins to suffer hallucinations, hearing thunder growl and echo across an immaculate sky, and even seeing swarms of birds describing strange patterns in the sky.

As a result of these dreams he becomes absorbed in a project that will cost him his job and his friends and will threaten his relationship: an extension of the storm shelter next to his house—an everyday attribute of dwellings in Ohio, a region frequently visited by tornados. In building up the shelter Curtis seeks to protect himself and his family, to confront a threat of another order and of which he is the prophet: an unprecedented unleashing of the elements, the end of the world. As his obsession gradually builds to the point where it becomes almost uncontrollable, in parallel Curtis tries to adopt the normative discourse of psychiatry, attempting to conserve, for better or worse, one foot in a real that is increasingly precarious and alien.

---

44.   Ibid., 95.

Although this personal and familial trial seems to recede after the quasi-imprisonment of his wife and son in the newly renovated shelter, LaForche, resting by the beach, then sees unfold before him, in the distance, an apocalyptic landscape, a host of approaching tornados, a vision he cannot dispel. But this tableau, which may just have been Curtis's nth hallucination, takes on an entirely other dimension when his son anxiously points out the storm unfurling in the distance, and his wife examines oily drops in the lines of her hand—raindrops exactly like those her husband had dreamt of, announcing the catastrophe to come.

From this contemporary tale we can extract a murky question: if the collapsing world vacillates firstly for ourselves and in ourselves, then at what point, and how, does hallucination turn into clairvoyance? For what is important in this film is not whether or not the final storm is real. The important point is that, whether or not the storm comes, the world is being experienced as a field of signs addressing themselves to it and for it. In this case, the question of whether or not Curtis is hallucinating does not *at all* alter his relation to the world. The world he represents to himself is a world that speaks to him, in this case traumatically. Whether such communication is a matter of phantasms or of a transcendent force makes no difference to his *experience* of it. The world is signalling to him.

What Nichols presents to us in this film is in fact nothing other than a contemporary variation on a theme that goes back to the dawn of humanity—the omen—updating it for a postmodern era prey to millennial fears, but which has forgotten how to live with them.

For the omen is always manifested by an aberration, a prodigy—that is to say, an inexplicable or incongruous event. Such an extraordinary happening can take various forms.

It could be, as related by Herodotus, a horse giving birth to a hare before Xerxes I, auguring an inevitable defeat; but it could also be the birth of a deformed baby or simply an unexpected meteorological phenomenon: an ill wind that unexpectedly rises, a bolt of lightning that comes from nowhere, or a prodigious storm that suddenly strikes can all suffice as a sign—for one who knows how to see it.

Thus, whether they are omens addressed to us, signs of divine anger, or resonances of the death of a supernatural being, abnormal or remarkable atmospheric phenomena, thunderstorms, fog, or storms can signal to the world of mortals events that are beyond them, but in which they have or will have, somehow, a role to play.

Through its natural manifestations, the environing world thus becomes a potential generator of messages that one must know how to decode: mantics, the art of divination, begins with the observation of the world so as to reveal its omens. It seeks its signs everywhere: in the entrails of animals (haruspicy), in the head of an ass thrown in the fire (cephalomancy), in the wind (anemomancy) or in lightning (brontomancy, practiced in the Etruscan world by specialized haruspices known as 'fulgurators')....

These precursor-signs, these messages concealed in the clouds or in a beast's entrails, confirm and reinforce the belief in an ordered world within which destiny and reasons may reveal themselves to those who know how to gather them, to one who knows how to uncover them, who knows where they are to be found. Knowledge of how to read them, how to decode the auguries, therefore procures such a figure unparalleled authority and prestige. Oracles know where others know nothing; and in virtue of this their predictions are incontestable. Incarnated in the Pythia of Delphi, for example, this power was a significant factor in the military and political decisions of Ancient Greece, demonstrating how the faculty of reading the unreadable and seeing the invisible can have an effective impact when it folds over onto the real world and exerts a determinative influence on it. If politics is based on the articulation of a *competence to see* and an *authority to speak*, then perhaps religion ultimately operates in a similar fashion, except that it is a matter of *seeing beyond the visible* and *translating the ineffable.*

The world of signs has no limits, and its manifestations are manifold. The omen, qua anomaly in the unrolling of a syntagmatic chain in Levi-Strauss's terms, or more prosaically a change in the order of things, however small, says nothing apart from this: the world is a world of laws, but these laws, though they may be unknown, do not fail to manifest themselves to us by way of various avatars.

Curtis LaForche lives in his environing world in a way that is not inherently different to that of a man living in Ancient Greece, apart from the fact that he belongs to a post-rationalist civilisation that has denied the omen and magical thought. He is therefore alone and helpless when faced with whatever it is that signals to him through atmospheric phenomena.

Combing the library in search of books on psychiatry in the hope of finding the key to decoding his psychoses, LaForche does not simply reveal himself as a wayward individual seeking an explanation for his illness; he also incarnates the debility of a normalised society when faced with syntagmatic ruptures. Despite his belief, despite his intuition, Curtis continues to conform to another credo, one deeply rooted and shared throughout society, and which dictates that he who uncovers an anomaly is doubtless himself, already, an anomaly. No doubt Curtis would prefer to be mad. No doubt that is, or would be, for himself and for those around him, a more bearable situation.

Faced with someone who claims to see and hear what no one else can perceive, the contemporary world has at its disposal only a simple, merciless alternative, divided between two poles: the subject in question is either a madman or a prophet. The over-rationalisation of our relation to the world has in effect, gradually but inexorably, engendered an unequivocal division of *murky factuality*, thereby denying its symbolic function, so as to integrate it *by force* into the reasoned concatenation of acts and things. And it is no exaggeration to ask whether such rationalisation of the sensible world, instigated by a will to enlighten the relation between man and world, has not, through its excess, played a part in the recrudescence of religious obscurantism, by de facto placing everything it cannot integrate on the side of the undecidable, and therefore the divine.

In other words, the abolition of magical thought, under the cosh of positivism, will have opened up an undivided reign for rational thought, either in the mode of an naturalist agnosticism, or through the prism of a religious dogma explaining everything except its own cause, that is to say its first or divine principle. For both approaches have a relation to the world that is similarly articulated: they decode the world of signs, discovering, representing, and communicating it, containing it within a convergent body of determinate, finite possibilities.

The world of signs is the theatre of operations wherein protocols of interpretation do battle. But beyond the macroscopic phenomena (dogmatisms, fanaticisms, prophetisms) that are sustained by and unfold from these discrete rootlets, their fibres take their nourishment from a more intimate loam,

which, although sometimes shared, can be experienced in an
entirely idiosyncratic way.

This vague space, which has always existed and which the
rational spirit has never managed entirely to annihilate, and
which, more often than we might imagine, sits as close as can
be to the advances of the enlightened spirit—as its shadow,
so to speak—is the space of superstition.

A SPECTRAL WORLD

Superstition is a modality of being-in-the-world. It is not an ad-hoc stringing together of more-or-less justified, more-or-less grounded beliefs, a rosary of faithless explanations. On the contrary, it is a tendency to believe that the world is irrigated by invisible forces, emerging and dissipating to the rhythm of ritual gestures and fortuitous coincidences. What this implies, ultimately, is that the world possesses an obscure side, which casts its invisible glimmer on the real, but whose interventions are knowable and avoidable—in short, it implies that an economy of the invisible is possible.

Malefic forces set their trap beneath a ladder because it forms a magical triangle with the wall and the floor; they incarnate themselves in a cat whose baleful power resides in the blackness of its pelt; they lie in wait in the fragile surface of a mirror which cannot be shattered without unpleasant consequences for the unlucky person who breaks it.

'We are not at home in this world.'[45] This sentence of August Strindberg's perfectly summarises the vexed situation of the superstitious person, warily negotiating a strange world, a world containing secrets no human will ever penetrate, yet whose effects make themselves known and can—indeed, must—be warded off.

Strindberg's superstition is most often stimulated by an attentive observation of phenomena that stand out to him. He moves vigilantly through life, on the lookout for signs concealed in commonplace occurrences. In his writing, the world of signs is always already an observable world, a world of sensible experience, that informs him of the machinations of his destiny. And these observations, this environment probed by

---

45.   A. Strindberg, *Journal Occulte, 1896–1908* (Paris: Mercure de France, 1971), 49.

the heightened sensibility of his dramaturgy, reveal hints of an unknown world which nevertheless makes itself apparent via singularities visible to anybody, but whose extraordinary character can only be detected by those who know how to observe. Thus, a certain cloud formation seems to present itself, year after year, for Strindberg's examination:

> For three years now, in the spring, the summer and the autumn, I have seen these same cloud-formations in a west or north-westly direction after sunset. I am beginning to think that these 'cloud-formations' must have a foundation in fact, for they are invariably the same. They must be optical illusions (or mirages) of places on the earth of which we know nothing. Swedenborg speaks of high places on the earth, unknown to us, where mighty beings dwell.[46]

In Strindberg's time, the world was not yet a finite surface where every fragment of land had been explored or photographed, but an unbounded space where uncharted domains, remote regions—unexplored and mysterious—and inaccessible lands inhabited by unknown beings were still a possibility.

This unknown space assumes a twofold function. Firstly, as a rationally, *geologically* existing locality, it folds the ensemble of unobservable possibilities reported in texts and legends onto itself, announcing, like the mirages observed by Strindberg, as-yet undiscovered lands. Secondly, it materialises a point at which the notion of a lacuna, a lack indicating an incomplete step in the long development of humankind's total

---

46.　A. Strindberg, *From an Occult Diary*, tr. M Sandbach (London: Secker & Warburg, 1965), 71.

knowledge of the world, may unfold. The blank space left on
the map, the *terra incognita*, is where we find the promise of
possible answers, making audible all that we have not yet
managed to comprehend, or even apprehend.

Often, in this way, the inexplicable nature of things demar-
cates a zone of rupture into which we can place the phantasmatic portion of the world, as humanity *believes* it to be. The
unknown world acts like a safety valve for the known world,
releasing into an imaginary place all that we have not yet managed to pacify, all that is still heterogeneous and illegitimate.
And the resulting two-sided world appears all the more real in
consigning this murky factuality to an unexplored grey zone
rather than allowing it to contaminate the known world, encir-
cling and returning to man. In this manner, Strindberg finds a
'real' cause for the formation of *imaginary* clouds, and sees
the real cause of cloud formation (the condensation of water
vapour in the air) as an *absence of cause*. And it is indeed an
absence of cause, for such a cause, in itself, *says* nothing, has
nothing to teach Strindberg about the horizon of his world,
which he ceaselessly interrogates.

Superstition, therefore, dreams of a vaster world for
humankind, a world that persists through and for, and even
beyond, the existence of man. A world that ultimately makes
sense and in which all mysteries find their solutions, even if
they are inaccessible. Superstition, following Theophrastus in
his *Characters*, comprises a fear of the gods, or more precisely, δεισιδαιμονία, a terror of the divine; a fear of invisible
spirits in general, and not simply of gods or demons.

In Strindberg's writings, spirits can be benevolent, such as
that of his third ex-wife who comes to visit him remotely, like
a succubus. But most often they are hostile, like the 'electri-
cians', the invisible yet assuredly human beings that oppress

him during his last visit to Paris, shocking him from afar with an electric current that grips his heart, every evening in bed, throughout the diverse crises endured throughout the Inferno period.

And in fact, this terror linked to electricity is not merely an idiosyncrasy of Strindberg's. A doctor friend even advised him never to mention it, at the risk of being committed, so recurrent was the theme of electricity, at the time, among the delirious episodes of the mentally estranged.

Electricity, the discovery of which was initially considered a minor affair pertaining solely to electrostatic phenomena, soon became an object of fascination (particularly once it was domesticated and introduced into the home), generating anxieties, fantasies, fears, and hopes that were never to be entirely defused.

In the journal *Le Grand Jeu*, dating from 1928, we find a striking example of the power of fascination concentrated in electrical phenomena:

> In April 1922 an engineer was visiting the workshops of the Thomas-Houston power plant. He was accompanied by a technician who was said to be the most reliable guide, having spent twenty years working in the plant and being therefore physically and mentally accustomed to operating in a state of constant alertness. However, in passing close by a high voltage wire, the technician informed his companion of the danger of approaching it, before suddenly reaching out and grasping it with his hand.[47]

To traverse and be traversed by an electric current. To participate in the becoming-energy of the world. To tear away the

---

47.   M. Lams, 'La tentation des volts', *Le Grand Jeu* 1 (Paris, 1928): 59–60.

veil of electricity's immateriality in order to feel it, to incorpo-
rate it, to be, in the words of Carlo Michelstaedter, *persuaded*.
Perhaps it works like this. Perhaps the technician wanted to
be persuaded *by* electricity, even if it cost him his life.

*

The experience of electricity was initially playful and light-
hearted. It coursed into the world of high society as a vitalising
force, a shiver running along the spine of social frivolities like
that of the conductive circle or, more intimately, electric kiss-
es.[48] But it was also an object of study, gradually but definitively accumulating an aura of great promise, especially in the
technical field. It was associated, furthermore, with mesmer-
ism, particularly in conjunction with the experimental valida-
tion of galvanism, or the possibility of interaction between
electrical currents and the living body.[49] Beyond simply delin-
eating a novel field of experimentation and scientific investigation, the discovery of electricity threw new light on the
question of materiality itself, liquefying the boundary between
matter and energy, solid structures and radiating forces, pul-
sations. The world became a beating heart, a space of circu-
lating flows.

This fascination with electricity should therefore not be
insulated from the interest which made it an object, during the

---

48.   Party games in which participants, holding hands in a circle or even
embracing, transfer an electric current from one to another. See *Revue des
Sciences Humaines* 281 (January–March 2006), 'L'imaginaire de l'électricité'.

49.   Indeed, during the Victorian era scientists went so far as to consider
the possibility of reanimating the dead through the application of electrical
currents to the brain, attempting to fulfil (while simultaneously disregarding
its warnings) the prophecy of Mary Shelley's pessimistic Promethean allegory
Frankenstein, written several decades earlier.

same period, of other theories revolving around research attempting to unveil the existence of invisible forces (Baron Reichenbach's *odic* forces, René Blondlot's 'N' rays), theories that were often combined more or less successfully with convincing experiments such as those carried out by Professor Röntgen, which would lead to the discovery of X-rays, radiography, and radiology. The world had suddenly become diaphanous—an architecture of translucent glass panes through which one was now able to peer.

One such discovery resulted in the possibility of photographing the invisible—a novel mode of capture capable of penetrating substance: for example, one could register the shape of a wristwatch hidden inside a wooden box. If the impact of the discovery of X-rays was so considerable, however, it was because it was applicable not only to inanimate objects, but also to the human body. Radiography produced a new, intermediate representation of the human form, simultaneously distinct from the depersonalised, anatomical image of the body without skin (if it is indeed still a body, no longer being graspable as an individual), and from that of the naked, physical body—painted, scrutinised, photographed—in which an integral mystery still endured, but only through a transposition of the body into an object of desire.

Hans Castorp, the protagonist of Thomas Mann's *The Magic Mountain*, is exposed to multiple radioscopic and radiographic procedures. Firstly as the anxious spectator of the electrochemical apparatus as it crackles into life, irradiating the room with the electrical forces it holds, tamed, within it; and then as a stirred witness to the disclosure of his cousin Joachim's torso—not without having asked in advance, out of modesty, for Joachim's permission to watch:

Hans Castorp peered through the pale window, peered into the void of Joachim Ziemssen's skeleton. His breastbone merged with his spine into one dark, gristly column. The ribs at the front of his rib cage overlapped those at the back, which looked paler. The collarbone curved upward on both sides, and the bones of the shoulder, the joint where Joachim's arm began, looked lean and angular against the soft halo of flesh. The chest cavity was bright, but one could make out a web of darker spots and black-ish ruffles. [...] But Hans Castorp was preoccupied with some-thing that looked like a sack, or maybe a deformed animal, visible behind the middle column, or mostly to the right of it from the viewer's perspective. It expanded and contracted regularly, like some sort of flapping jellyfish.

'Do you see his heart?' the director asked [...]. Good God, it was his heart, Joachim's honour-loving heart, that Hans Castorp saw.

'I can see your heart,' he said in a choked voice.[50]

There is no doubt that the experience has made a profound impression on the young Castorp. It is indeed an X-ray—the token of ultimate intimacy—that he will beg for and receive as a gift from his fellow sanatorium resident Clawdia Chauchat, with whom he has been in love since the beginning, and who agrees, for a single night only, and just before departing, to be his mistress.

There is indeed something intimate about the act of look-ing *inside* a living being, of seeing their spectre. Something rare, forbidden, sacrilegious even. Something which, by its very nature, draws one closer and alienates one at the same time. Is there anything more intimate than visual contact with the

50.   T. Mann, *The Magic Mountain* [1924], tr. J.E. Woods (New York: Vintage, 1996), 214–15.

beating heart of one's relative, or the inside of a lover's chest? And yet what an insurmountable distance, impossible to diminish, separates these two states—that of the cousin or the lover, and that of these ghostly dematerialised bodies. Such a connection evokes the *telephonic* subsistence of the Duchampian body—which proposes, as a method of exempting oneself from military service, a becoming-deferred of the body and the communication of its parts 'from one deferee to another'.[51]

Radiography gives rise to just such a form of intimacy, penetrating a soft envelope of flesh only to disclose an unattainable 'deferee'. It produces a conjunction of antithetical elements, setting them out in a paradoxical arrangement: X-rays pierce the body, cutting across its surface to generate a kind of abstraction, an absence; but they also reveal the skeletal structure, sometimes even the organs, thus reducing the body, momentarily evaporated and sublimed, to its organic architecture, a body-machine completely subordinated to the laws of physics and biology. What X-rays reveal is a body simultaneously diaphanous and structured, a body whose volumes are dissipated in order to unveil its architectural laws, a body in which the soul, invisible, can no longer hide itself, effaced by the means of its transparent disclosure.

But for Castorp, when it is his own body that is being scrutinised, this moving, intimate, vivid experience is reduced to a macabre omen—an implacable memento mori reminding

---

51.   'Against compulsory military "service": a "*deferment*" of each limb, of the heart and the other anatomical parts; each soldier being already unable to put his uniform on again, his heart feeding *telephonically*, a deferred arm, etc. *Then*, no more feeding; each "*deferee*" isolating himself. Finally a Regulation of regrets from *one "deferee" to another*.' M. Duchamp, 'Deferment', in M. Sanouillet and E. Peterson (eds.), *The 1914 Box*, *Salt Seller: The Essential Writings of Marcel Duchamp*, (London: Thames and Hudson, 1975), 23.

him of the inevitability of his own death, affirming that alterity within himself via the manifestation of his own becoming-spectral. 'Spooky, isn't it? Yes, there's no mistaking that whiff of spookiness', confirms the sanatorium's Director Behrens, Castorp's doctor.

The investigation into the invisible face of the world raised a dust cloud of ideas and intuitions that continues to bloom under the patronage of a purely rational methodology. From the enthusiasm provoked by novel modes of capture and unveiling, in particular those enabled by the advent of techniques for the reproduction of the sensible, there flowed a belief that the invisible, and even the afterlife, were within reach of our instruments.

It is not by chance that one finds respected inventors, responsible for discoveries that played key roles in the modification of the sensible world—whether by solidifying the technologies that supported its reproduction (phono-, photo-, and cinematography) or by exposing previously unknown layers of reality (X-rays)—among the proponents of psychical research. From William Crookes, inventor of a vacuum tube that led to the discovery of X-rays, to Oliver Lodge, developer of the principle of syntony for radio (as well as a teacher and indefatigable defender of spiritualism), passing, notably, by way of the great Edison, who experimented with the possibility of communication between the living and the dead, diverse lines of enquiry, emanating from the fringes of the twentieth century, converged to penetrate the known world via the flourishing of new media, so as to illuminate its thickness—just as a body exposed to X-rays reveals an unsuspected aspect of the complex prism we call 'reality'.

*

The discovery of invisible forces (X-rays, electricity) and the technical reproduction of the sensible contributed to the unfolding of the known world. These innovations reaffirmed the belief in a world that had yet to reveal all of its secrets, a world that humankind, lacking a sufficiently complex sensorium, was unable to fully apprehend without the aid of tools or protocols suited to the task.

These novel techniques appeared to herald the dawn of a renewed age whose obscure face, invisible yet irresistibly close, pulsed continuously, projecting its dark rays in every direction. Like a sombre lake, the world intimated the promise of unsounded depths. An unknown expanse, diffuse and translucent, poised to appear at any moment, absent yet always already there. It was therefore necessary to persevere in the work of tearing away the veil of the known world, of *augmenting it*, as it were, and to plunge ever deeper into these mysterious regions, even if this meant employing unprecedented experimental methods at odds with the conventions of orthodox science. So it was that spiritualism, with its table-tapping, ouija boards, mediums, and photographic instruments, played its part in the discovery of the spectral world.

The spectral world is the world revealed as a site traversed by fluid forces. This world on the very brink of perception, which some claim to have conquered, is the destination of all our fantasies. It suggests, and announces itself as, an outside. And it is by way of manifestations, channelling, and suggestion that the spiritualists attempt to connect the world of the living to the world of the dead, or more precisely, to re-establish the unity of these two worlds. For the spectral world is not the world of the dead. Nor is a spectre a dead person, but the animated and energetic manifestation of a being that no longer belongs to the world of the living. Spiritualism posits the existence of an immaterial world beyond appearance, where an economy of invisible energies pulses in defiance of death. This is where the ghosts reside, impalpable yet present. They haunt the material world, moving in accordance with the flux of mysterious currents. What spiritualism proposes to do, therefore, is to find methods for receiving these emanations, notably through the aid of mediums, operating as 'antennae' attuned to the frequencies of the ghosts so as to actualise them in the material world.

In spiritualism, ghosts, spectres, and mysterious forces— an entire ephemeral and translucent universe—were able to assume for the first time, under the administration of pseudo-scientific methodologies, a quasi-concrete, quasi-objective status, calling attention to a strange traffic that circulated everywhere, blurring the material boundaries between bodies and things just as it blurred the threshold between the perceived world and the real world.

It is the province of the spectral world to draw the contour of this limit-point, this knot of confusion between the world of facts and the world of dreams, which reciprocally cut across one another to form the world of lived experience. In this respect, the spectral world is an *imaginary* world. This assertion, needless to say, does not answer the question of the reality or facticity of such a world. To be precise, the interlacing of the spectral world with an imaginary dimension renders its status undecidable. Indeed it is the conviction that 'reality' or 'facticity' can be clearly designated that itself vacillates.

Perhaps the pursuit of the spectral world can be extended by endeavours to modify the supposedly deficient—or at least limited—human sensorium. In a short story entitled 'From Beyond', written in 1920, Howard Phillips Lovecraft alludes to this sensory insufficiency, imagining a machine capable of augmenting our perceptual capacities:

> What do we know [...] of the world and the universe about us? Our means of receiving impressions are absurdly few, and our notions of surrounding objects infinitely narrow. We see things only as we are constructed to see them, and can gain no idea of their absolute nature. With five feeble senses we pretend to comprehend the boundlessly complex cosmos, yet other beings with a wider, stronger, or different range of senses might not only see very differently the things we see, but might see and study whole worlds of matter, energy, and life which lie close at hand yet can never be detected with the senses we have. I have always believed that such strange, inaccessible worlds exist at our very elbows, and now I believe I have found a way to break down the barriers. I am not joking. Within twenty-four hours that machine near the table will generate waves acting on unrecognised sense-organs that exist in us as atrophied or rudimentary vestiges. Those waves will open up to us many vistas unknown to man, and several unknown to anything we consider organic life. We shall see that at which dogs howl in the dark, and that at which cats prick up their ears after midnight. We shall see these things, and other things which no breathing creature has yet seen. We shall overleap time, space, and dimensions, and without bodily motion peer to the bottom of creation.[52]

In this story, Lovecraft envisions a strange machine capable of emitting waves which stimulate unknown sense-organs, igniting a latent human ability to perceive alternative dimensions of reality.

---

52.   H.P. Lovecraft, 'From Beyond', in *H.P. Lovecraft Omnibus 2: Dagon and Other Macabre Tales* (London: HarperCollins, 2000), 90.

These imaginary organs bring to mind the pineal gland, vestigial organ of the parietal eye, also known as the 'third eye' in reference to the extra-sensory capacities that have been attributed to it. Here Lovecraft combines two approaches: the tendency, discussed above, to place technical discoveries at the centre of new protocols of sensation, and the now outmoded inclination to see the human being as an incipient species whose evolutionary potential has yet to fully unfold.

There are multiple theories concerning the third eye, from symbolic interpretations that understand it as a kind of self-awareness or inner vision, to more literal interpretations that connect it to the pineal gland, and treat it as a kind of psychic receiver. This gland, which for Descartes was the 'seat of the soul', and whose principle function is to secrete melatonin, plays an important role in the regulation of biological rhythms. The pineal eye was also an object of reflection—or better, of fantasy—for Georges Bataille, who characterised it as the sense-organ linked to the erection of a vertical 'system of impulsions'. To this idealised, vertical, pineal vision, Bataille opposes a horizontal, binocular vision. This latter corresponds to the world of reason, 'a real world of utility', as he will later put it, enabling us to understand the space within which we have evolved. The former, more mysterious, latent, turned toward the heavens—and more specifically, toward the Sun[53]—is meant to support man in his vertical dimensionality, equally chthonic and celestial.

---

53. 'Virtual vision, of which the pineal gland is the organ, can be defined as the vision of the celestial vault in general, but since the different angles of the vault are not equal among themselves, given the movement and increase in intensity of the solar centre which determines it throughout the day in relation to the zenith, it is feasible to take the sun at the meridian as the essential object of the virtual eye.' G. Bataille, 'Dossier de l'œil pinéal', in Œuvres complètes II: Écrits posthumes 1922–1940 (Paris: Gallimard, 1970), 39.

Although symbolically linked to Bataille's personal mythology, this vision is not exclusively metaphorical. For Bataille recognizes that he had called this pineal vision, virtual until then, into being:

> During this period [1927], I did not hesitate to think seriously of the possibility that this extraordinary eye would finally really come to light through the bony roof of the head, because I believed it necessary that, after a long period of servility, human beings would have an eye just for the sun (whereas the two eyes in their sockets turn away from it with a kind of stupid obstinacy). I was not insane but I made too much of the necessity of leaving, in one way or another, the limits of our human experience, and I adapted myself in a fairly disordered way so that the most improbable thing in the world (the most overwhelming as well, something like foam on the lips) would at the same time appear to me to be necessary.[54]

Such an eye, Bataille ended up having to admit, would never be likely to erupt from the human skull. Yet it was still suspected to exist, only 'inwardly turned' and hence potentially capable of modulating perception. Numerous attempts to explain the mechanism of altered perception connected to the use of drugs make mention of the pineal gland, which secretes a hormone derived from serotonin, a neurotransmitter that itself appears to be altered by the absorption of psychotropics such as LSD and mescaline.

A great many theories concerning psychedelia see the pineal gland/eye as the key to opening the *doors of*

---

54.   G. Bataille, 'The Jesuve', in *Visions of Excess: Selected Writings 1927–1939*, tr. A. Stoekl (Minneapolis: University of Minnesota Press, 1985), 74–5.

perception, to borrow the title of Aldous Huxley's text. One of the principle theses of that essay, referencing the work of Bergson, is that our operational consciousness of the world— that which orients us and synchronises us with reality—is a limited, discontinuous, and 'reductive' consciousness, attuned only to objects structured by symbolisation and language. According to Huxley, the effect of psychotropics unbridles this consciousness, giving us access the world in all its plenitude:

> To be shaken out of the ruts of ordinary perception, to be shown for a few timeless hours the outer and the inner world, not as they appear to an animal obsessed with survival or to a human being obsessed with words and notions, but as they are appre- hended, directly and unconditionally, by Mind at Large—this is an experience of inestimable value to everyone.[55]

*

Whatever the means may be—communication with spirits, more or less phantasmatic scientific techniques capable of revealing the invisible world, machines or substances that activate and extend the human sensorium—it is always the same sentiment that presides over their implementation: a sense of the world's incompleteness, or more precisely, the incompleteness of our perception of it.

It is evidently quite a seductive notion that such incomple- tion can be overcome by these external elements that stimu- late our senses and our imagination. But undoubtedly this is a kind of short cut, or a short-circuit, which takes visions sug- gestive of another world for tangible evidence of its existence,

---

55.   A. Huxley, 'The Doors of Perception', in *The Doors of Perception and Heaven and Hell* (London: Penguin, 1971), 60.

in so far as these protocols have recourse to subjective judgment and an 'inner world'. For example, those who have suffered the loss of a loved one are among the most ardent defenders of spiritualism. This point can be illustrated with two famous cases: Oliver Lodge, who lost his son Raymond in the war, aged only twenty-six, and Victor Hugo, whose daughter Léopoldine drowned at nineteen years of age. Having been put in contact with their lost children, both Lodge and Hugo attested to the possibility of communication between the world of the living and that of the dead. The doors to the unknown world swing open more frequently when questions or intuitions harden into convictions, when the desire to believe becomes irresistible. So it is the imagination, above all, that contributes to the unveiling of the world, because it is the imagination that procures its 'proofs'.

It would therefore be ill-advised to attempt to establish a neat division between the real and the imaginary world. The imaginary world, the world of phantasms, exists only in relation to the real world, only as a resonance, extending, replacing, or even banishing it rather than negating it pure and simple. If Lovecraft conjures pagan horrors and ancestral abominations, he does so in order to exorcise an exterior world and a society that terrifies him, having become too heterogeneous. The imagination, as the manufacturer of representations, can thus prove an eminently conservative device, smuggling in representations of the world that serve to make it more bearable.

Rather than distinguishing the real from the imaginary, we should instead affirm the imaginary modality of the real world. Such a world oscillates continuously between two poles: that of the 'visible', verifiable, reproducible, and certain, and that of the invisible, conjectural, hypothetical, and imaginary. These two poles are not antagonistic, they do not work against one another. On the contrary, they complement and nourish one another. They conspire to structure a murky factuality, to bring about the observable vacillations of the real. They balance the subtle pressure of the spectral world, like a safety valve that is necessary in order for us to accept the concrete world and to inscribe ourselves within it. They *define* it.

If the infiltration of the spectral world benefits the real world, it does so by inhibiting its univocity, to the extent that it was possible in the first place. It solidifies the real, explains it, or, more precisely, it domesticates the inexplicable (albeit explicable) spaces of the real by rendering them *mundane*. Superstition, which, to reiterate, is a modality of being-in-the-world, resorts to a symbolic register and integrates murky factuality into an economy that is familiar and local: death or the fear of annihilation, incarnated as a malevolent spirit or evil eye, can then be temporarily banished by throwing a pinch of salt over one's shoulder. It is by means of these small victories over the invisible world, fought and won on the terrain of the real, that one gains mastery over one's own life—destabilised by the unknown but inscribed in a tangible locality.

The spectral world is not, therefore, a pure origin, a terra incognita, the virgin zone on a map labelled 'hic sunt dracones'. It is an accumulation of forgotten things, of losses which continue to make themselves manifest, lingering behind. It is an intermediate space, a space of disappearance and of survival. A spectral world—ghostly, because it can never be actualised. For a ghost is an entity *whose apparition is not a presence*.

The spectral world is the world of signs gone mad. A world where a symbol produces an event, where imagination becomes perception. It is a splintered world where the frontier dividing the living from the dead is porous. It is the *interworld*, running along the edge of the Styx, the Acheron, the world through which the strange figure in the canoe of Peter Doig's painting *100 Years Ago* drifts. A shore at which it is impossible to dock. Unless, perhaps, the 'hauntology' touched upon by Derrida means this: tethering oneself to the unstable banks of the spectral world, not to study its contours but to adopt its point of view.

Finally, the spectral world is a world barely afloat, moored to the world of dreams, pulling against the world of utility, contesting it while simultaneously extending it and ceaselessly returning to it. And yet sometimes it almost wrenches itself entirely free. Sometimes imagination founders. Sometimes superstition comes to a standstill. Sometimes the world of representations is saturated. One final example: Lovecraft, as we said, wards off the real with monstrous visions. But sometimes he pushes the imagination to its limits, to the point where the abominations become *indescribable*, where words cannot delineate these creatures that are no longer monsters, but horror itself. In doing so he indicates not a world beyond imagination, but a world *beneath* it.

Beneath, there is another world, utterly removed from any imaginable world, as distant as possible from any exotic land. A land where no dragons hide.

THE INFRA-WORLD

The world cannot be replaced by its representation. This is what is revealed by the vacillation of the sensible, by our uncertainty when confronted with borderline-forms. There is always a remainder, a surplus that runs through us and insinuates itself into our relation with the world, without ever submitting itself to identification, without ever taking on sufficient form to be named.

This un-presentable quantity is that which refuses all formalisation, every attempt to put it into words. It is the infrasensible yet still sensible manifestation of an ineffable space where nothing is said and everything is sensed. One famous and peculiar text gives us an admirable illustration of emergent defiance in the face of the words of the world. This short yet decisive work is the *Letter of Lord Chandos*, written by Hugo von Hofmannsthal and published in 1902. It was supposedly penned, as the title indicates, by Phillip Lord Chandos—a fictional character said to be the son of the Count of Bath—and is addressed to the famous philosopher Francis Bacon (1561–1626).

In this letter (which would be his last) Chandos attempts, as best as he can, to explain, or more precisely to sensitise his correspondent to, the reasons behind his renunciation of writing. For, despite being the author of noteworthy works in his youth, he has lost his ability with words. It is not so much that he has forgotten them, or that they have deserted him, rather it is as if he has pierced through them, traversing their surface significations only to discover nothing, a void. Henceforth, 'the abstract terms of which the tongue must avail itself as a matter of course in order to voice a judgment, crumbled in [his] mouth like mouldy fungi.'[56]

---

56.   H. von Hofmannsthal, 'Letter of Lord Chandos', tr. T. and J. Stern, in J. D. McClatchy (ed.), *The Whole Difference: Selected Writings of Hugo Von Hofmannsthal* (Princeton: Princeton University Press, 2008), 73.

Every utterance, every judgment of value, will become for him a source of indefinable malaise, revealing in each affirmation its 'mendacious' character, 'indemonstrable', 'as hollow as could be', and rendering him incapable of *authoritative* speech— that is to say, of the ability to be certain of anything at all—so fiercely do words now seem to have been emptied of all meaning.

It is as if Chandos is unable to distance himself from the world that surrounds him; his mind compels him 'to view all things which occur [...] from an uncanny closeness. [...] I no longer succeeded', he writes, 'in comprehending them with the simplifying eye of habit. Everything disintegrated into parts, those parts again into parts; no longer would anything let itself be encompassed by one idea.'[57] Estranged from himself, Chandos becomes subject to unsettling sensible experiences provoked by nothing, or very little:

> [O]n finding beneath a nut tree a half-filled pitcher which a gardener boy had left there, and the pitcher and the water in it, darkened by the shadow of the tree, and a beetle swimming on the surface from shore to shore, this combination of trifles sent through me such a shudder at the presence of the Infinite, a shudder running from the roots of my hair to the marrow of my heels. What was it that made me want to break into words which, I know, were I to find them, would force to their knees those cherubim in whom I do not believe? What made me turn silently away from this place? Even now, after weeks, catching sight of that nut tree, I pass it by with a shy sidelong glance, for I am loath to dispel the memory of the miracle hovering there

57.   Ibid., 74.

round the trunk, loath to scare away the celestial shudders that still linger about the shrubbery in this neighbourhood.[58]

Chandos is no longer the author of these perceptual representations. He submits to them and receives their impact in an unmediated fashion, in a purely *pathic* manner, without any discursive filter to condition them or put them into perspective—without, very precisely, anything to distance them from him. Thus opening his being to the ineffable, Chandos is confronted with two indissociable experiences: that of a defiance of language, the protocol for encoding his relationship with the real, and that of a *pathic fascination*.

More than ten years before writing this text, Hofmannsthal reveals to his friend, Edgar Karg, in a genuine letter, certain conceptions which will later find their expression in 'Chandos syndrome':

> [M]ost people do not live in life, but in a simulation, a sort of algebra where nothing *exists* and everything simply *signifies*. [...] The vertiginous-being of mountains, the immense-being of the sea, the obscure-being of the night, the way horses stare, the shape of our hands, the scent of carnations [...]: in all the innumerable things of existence, individually in each and in a singular fashion, something immune to being rendered in words but which speaks to our souls, expresses itself.[59]

The character of Chandos also identifies a state of affairs preceding his crisis, wherein each thing seems to be in its place,

---

58.   Ibid., 76 [translation modified].

59.   H. von Hofmannsthal, 'Lettre à Edgar Karg, juin 1895', in *Lettres de Lord Chandos* (Paris: Gallimard, 1980), 223.

where each constitutive element of the world possesses meaning, not so much in itself, but for the person who observes it, who will be able, if need be, to *use* it:

> [I]n a state of continuous intoxication, I conceived the whole of existence as one great unit: the spiritual and physical worlds seemed to form no contrast, as little as did courtly and bestial conduct, art and barbarism, solitude and society; in everything I felt the presence of Nature. [...] I divined that all was allegory and that each creature was a key to all the others; and I felt myself the one capable of seizing each by the handle and unlocking as many of the others as were ready to yield.[60]

But the world that Chandos will perceive from this moment onward is a world of effaced signs. The self-estrangement he undergoes—identifying himself, for example, with the rats dying from the effects of the poison he had previously given orders to distribute—goes hand in hand with the implosion of a language tasked with accounting for every thing.

In another letter to Edgar Karg, written several days after the one cited above, Hofmannsthal attests to this terminal impossibility of *speaking the world*:

> Words do not belong to this world, they belong to a world of the self, a complete and total world like the world of sound. We can speak everything that exists and we can put everything that exists into music. But we can never fully say what a thing is as it is. This is why poetry arouses a sterile nostalgia, just like sound.

---

60.   Hofmannsthal, 'Letter of Lord Chandos', 71–2 [translation modified].

A lot of people do not know this and almost lose themselves in wanting to make life speak.[61]

And yet the aim is always to *speak* the world, even if only to constitute it as a world. The world *qua world* is born of a process of elaboration, an all-encompassing strategy that is precisely a strategy of language. In a work entitled, incidentally, *Speak the World*, Francis Wolff focuses on the joint between perception and language, showing how one belongs to the domain of the particular and the local, the other to that of the general and the communal, and how, in order to *function*, one cannot do without the other. Perception requires stable categories into which to insert its data in order for them be communalised, formalised, and exchanged, as it were, within an economy of sense. Meanwhile, language utilises perceptual matter as raw material for the development of the categories (words) that will constitute it.

The permanence of the world is premised on the smooth functioning of this joint. In order to 'make the world', as Wolff writes, the perceived must fit into the world's space of non-contradiction, a space in which the only inviolable law is that, if a thing is a thing (which is to say, *designated* as that which it is), it cannot be another thing at the same time. Furthermore, in order for the perceived to become a thing (the object of a designation), it must first of all be 'qualified', or decanted from an ensemble of perceptions. It must take on form.[62]

---

61.   H. von Hofmannsthal, *Les mots ne sont pas de ce monde: lettres à un officier de marine* (Paris: Payot et Rivages, 2005), 126–7.

62.   'The perceived', writes Wolff, 'does not "make up" a world, because what it lacks is everything belonging, together, as part of the same construction [...] along with objective exteriority structured in concepts by the communalisation of experience.' F. Wolff, *Dire le monde* (Paris: PUF, 1997), 27.

This forming of the sensible, or 'clarification' to use Weininger's term, is already inherent to the strategies of language. The basis of language, if we are to believe Saussure, is established in the identification of similarity and difference, and in their ratification. But, as has been argued above, such a procedure degrades primary experience by *conditioning* it. As Francis Wolff maintains,

> the essential thing is that we are able to speak. For, being able to speak to one another, to speak of things infinitely and to be able to speak infinitely otherwise, to be able to contradict ourselves in relation to a non-contradictory world, comes at this price: never knowing truly, completely, what things are or why they are what they are.[63]

This comes back to the fact that the world is already a 'language-world', that the making of the world is always already organized around identified and qualified sensations. To the question 'What must the world be in order for us to be able to speak it?', Wolff responds, 'a total order regarding that which can be submitted to reason [and] a common order regarding that which can be exchanged'.[64]

If perception is a sieve, what can be said of that which slips through its net, how does one speak of what escapes? What remains of unqualified perceptions, of vanishing sensations, these scarcely noticeable, faintly sketched things? What is their influence and their effect upon us? Where do the indescribable, nocturnal fears hide, the horrors lurking behind closed eyes, the epiphany experienced by Chandos at the

---

63.   Ibid., 81.

64.   Ibid. 27–33.

sight of a watering can forgotten beneath a tree? What sub-terranean economy weaves itself beneath the making of the world? What of the world beneath language? What of the infra-world?

*

In a video work entitled *The Night Watch*, Belgian artist Francis Alÿs releases a fox named Bandit overnight in a deserted National Portrait Gallery. With the help of surveillance cameras installed in each room, the artist shows us the nocturnal comings and goings of the animal, left to itself in the London museum.

By means of this procedure, Alÿs allows us to observe a reconfiguration of the functional and sensible space of the exhibition. The fox paces up and down the corridors, sniffs about, climbs into a display case to rest in safety, and comprehends things that are absent from our senses. It moves about the space following its own laws, dictated by its apprehension of the surrounding environment, or what Jakob von Uexküll termed its 'milieu'.[65] Its movements are guided by sensory currents comprising odours unavailable to human sensible apprehension, leading it from room to room, proposing U-turns and retracings of steps, generating a true infra-sensible network.

But this reconfiguration of space resides no less in the revelation of a world unfolding beneath our sensory capacities than in that which evades the apprehension of the fox itself: not only does Bandit ignore the paintings (it has never learned to look at them), it also roams the museum in an impossible manner, improper to the primary function of the premises—

---

65.   See J. von Uexküll, *A Foray into the Worlds of Animals and Humans*, tr. J.D. O'Neil (Minneapolis: University of Minnesota Press, 2010).

which is designed to be a space for passing through, structured by organised, sequenced stops—a transitional space. The back-and-forth of the fox suppresses the navigational currents proper the museum, its *logic*. Bandit does not see the museum. It wanders in an undefined space that is also a space whose possibilities have not yet been determined by use—a space of invention, as it were.

To learn how to look and listen is equally to learn how to be blind and deaf to what it is not apposite to see or hear. It is a process of rendering the world mute. The fox advances through an ineffable world, but it is nevertheless a living world possessed of a thickness, a mysteriousness, unknown elements and magical milieux.[66] In sum, this is a world that the fox itself *does not know* but in which it has learned to live, yet it is equally a world that the fox suppresses or is partially ignorant of. In *The Nightwatch*, the thickness of the unknown is flipped, transforming the objects familiar to man (the paintings) into elements that are strictly invisible for the fox.

Although they are not random, although they are determined by the environment, the movements of the fox are not relics of a sense forgotten by man and to which he has lost access. To think like this would be to attempt to find a way to *make* the animal *speak*, as in the Dogon 'fox divination' ritual. The ritual makes use of a grid—a large rectangle framed by stones, made up of squares drawn on the ground by the diviner, beyond the boundary of the village. Each square contains symbols and sticks distributed by the diviner according to the questions of the person on whose behalf the ritual is being performed. Before leaving the ritual site until the following day, this person must throw a handful of peanuts onto the grid.

66.   Ibid., 120.

During the night, a fox will come to eat them, disturbing the marks drawn on the ground. The next morning, returning to the site, the diviner observes the traces left by the animal in the different squares and interprets them, using the information to predict the future, thanks to the secret message delivered by the fox.

But Bandit is not an instrument of divination. Its movements inside the museum are not destined for the symbolic space of portents. The fox ranges across the ineffable, the mute terrain of Chandos's experience. It does not reveal anything of a higher world in its ambulations. On the contrary, it navigates the infra-world, a world not yet composed of certitudes, an errant world of forgetfulness and fleeting overtures. And this free navigation, gratuitous and disordered, is infinitely more unsettling and subversive than if the animal were to stop before the paintings to contemplate them, or, like the Dogon fox, to transmit a prophecy through its wanderings.

The fantasy of a secret authoritative role consecrated to animals as the bearers of hidden truths can be also be found in a childhood memory of W.G. Sebald, recounted in *The Rings of Saturn*, a memory which recalls an ancient omen in which the 'courses' drawn by flocks of birds delineate a meaningful world:

> At earlier times, in the summer evenings during my childhood when I had watched from the valley as swallows circled in the last light, still in great numbers in those days, I would imagine that the world was held together by the courses they flew through the air.[67]

---

67.   W. G. Sebald, *The Rings of Saturn* [1995], tr. M. Hulse (London: Vintage, 2002), 67.

All things considered, it is more reassuring to regard the flight of birds or the path of a fox as a kind of coded message from higher forces, intended to communicate something to us, than to understand them as an autonomous existence with its own logic and ends that we strictly cannot appreciate, the action of strange beings upon our vision of the world, beings who absolutely refuse to share that vision, and yet inhabit the same space, the same time, in a parallel world, as it were: a world constituted by their own unique perceptions and affects.

This anxiety implicitly reveals an impenetrable, chthonic world, in opposition to the harmonious and ethereal world in which every gesture and every word would be the extension of a harmonic order, a beacon of this order which begins and ends with man. Such egocentrism is not culpable in itself. It is a natural response. Everyone must constitute themselves as being-in-the-world and, in order to do so, it is necessary to structure the world for oneself. Once again, this is the link that crumbles for Chandos, the link between the affirmation of an ordered world and the assumption of personal finitude. This frontier, furthermore, continually exposes its artificiality (which is not at all trivial) to the minds of those who undertake the task of constructing or reconstructing the world for themselves, as in pathological cases for example, or even in childhood.

*

A friend related to me a memory of a game he used to play as a child. At the age of about seven, in the town square of a little village in Corrèze, he would throw a hoop to entertain himself, aiming for the bollards that demarcated the square. In his imagination, each bollard symbolised one of the ordering forces of the world, such as Nature, the Divine, or even his own mind. In throwing the hoop over each bollard, he tried, as part of the game, to influence the conditions of his path through life. Thus the world presented itself to him as having an inflection point, an adjustable variable with which he could interact by means of a ritual operation. This childhood game enabled him to construct the world he lived in, and even his future place in that world, thanks to a set of abstract concepts that had previously been passed on to him and which he had already started to put to use.

This practice of intervening in an ordered world can also be observed in certain pathologies. Acting on the world and maintaining its stability is a method for the psychotic, who attempts to erect an order in a similar fashion to the child, for the purpose of structuring the world and locating themselves within it, seeking a way to maintain unity against a tendency to dissolution and molecularisation in a world that is itself already split.

In his work *Creation and Schizophrenia*,[68] Jean Oury provides, among others, two particularly lucid examples. The first concerns a paraphrenic patient named Mister X. One day Mister X ran away. He was later discovered, stretched out in a ditch on the side of a road. He refused to move, explaining: 'No, no, no, I am here to feed all the animals of the earth with my blood.' Mister X had taken on the quasi-sacrificial responsibility of feeding the world's animals, and had to remain in a specific place in order to fulfil his task. The second case described by Oury involves a patient of the Saint-Alban psychiatric hospital named Arthur:

---

68.   J. Oury, *Création et Schizophrénie* (Paris: Galilée, 1989).

Arthur spent his days next to a wall, beneath a drainpipe that had been leaking for years. Drop after drop, incessantly; moss had grown on the wall. [...] Beneath the drainpipe, in a rhythmic fashion, he turned round and round. [...] He had a responsibility even greater than that of giving his blood to the animals: he was responsible for the rotation of the earth. If he stopped, the earth stopped. To justify this, he had explained that Saint-Alban was situated on a ridgeline dividing three river basins. This is true: the Cantal, the Margeride, and the Cévennes. One side flows towards the Mediterranean, the other towards the Atlantic. He was, therefore, master of dividing the waters.[69]

Acting on the order of the world—being responsible for its structure and its durability, whether by assuring the rotation of the planet or the sustenance of its animals—is an oblique means of constructing a self, of reconstituting it, or rather *reinstating* it, as a being-in-the-world. To provide for the world of signs by playing a major role in it, whether by helping to keep it in order or, more simply, by observing how this order manifests itself, amounts to the same thing: warding off the infra-world.

Because, everywhere, at every moment, it is unravelling. Everywhere, it oozes, it crouches in the shadows. Beneath language, beneath sensations. A quaking world. The infra-world is not a speculative reality. It is the mute and blind portion of the real, its accursed share. It is the world of exiled impressions and actions, but it is not an absent world. The infra-world is the world that withdraws from the infraliminal world of perception. It is what fails to make a world.

69.   Ibid., 126.

The infra-world is the milieu of unobjectivated sensations and unconscious impressions, of occurrences barely remarked (or insufficiently remarked to be remembered). The territories concealed by sensation are vast. Their administration is perilous and fragile. Even so, the sensible is not reducible to its formulation. It is in its resistance to the formulations of the sensible that the infra-world persists. Every sensation contains an un-presentable element that remains immune to perceptual neutralization and is simply masked. In this way, the space of the sensible always exceeds the space of representation.

The infra-world is no less effective for being hidden. It generates effects, it reverberates through our sensations, our decisions, and our actions. It shapes our social and emotional lives. It speaks beneath words, but it is not the bearer of truth or authority. For if language *makes* the world, the infra-world is the place where language is *absent*—the receptacle of the world's remainder. It is the part divested of language, the keeper of invisible shocks, of lives not lived, aborted projects, non-events, realities struggling to come into being.

The infra-world, finally, is the world of impaired imagination, imagination being understood not as an evasion of the real but, on the contrary, as an integral part of its construction. For a dream world or an imaginary world is still a world of signs, a realisable world. The infra-world, on the other hand, is imageless; nothing can construct itself there. It inheres in formlessness, silence, and utter darkness. It does not reflect on itself, it reveals itself only in the hollows and the cracks of thought, in the blind spots of perception. Through it, the world of the real-immutable order of things is refuted.

The infra-world is available only to an infra-lucidity. If extra-lucidity discovers signs where no one else sees them, infra-lucidity is something else, a certain sentiment, an inclination to plunge beneath the surface of things, a suspicion that every phenomenon, as exceptional or prodigious as it may be, is not fundamentally distinguishable from the most anodyne fact. And that the most banal, anodyne fact harbours an abyss that one risks sinking into at every instant. Chandos is the very figure of the infra-lucid, the inverted clairvoyant who is no longer able to convince himself of the validity of anything, who is incapable of erecting even the most minimal authoritative scaffolding.

Infra-lucidity pays no attention to ghosts or to that which returns from the dead. It does not see omens in the trajectory of a flock of birds. But it senses, at every instant, the silent rustling of the infra-world.